The AI Freelancer

Leveraging Artificial Intelligence to Boost Your Writing Career

Florence De Borja

Contents

Introduction

Welcome to the Future of Freelance Writing

Technological advancements are continuously molding the dynamic terrain of freelance writing, driving its evolution. From the clattering keys of typewriters to the sleek efficiency of modern laptops, the tools of the trade have drastically transformed, enabling writers to adapt and thrive. This exploration delves into the rich history of freelance writing, the digital revolution's profound impact, and AI's crucial role in enhancing productivity and competitiveness.

The Evolution of Freelance Writing

Freelance writing has come a long way from the days of typewriters. These mechanical marvels, first commercialized by Christopher Latham Sholes in the 1860s, revolutionized writing by offering unprecedented speed and legibility (*The Development*, n.d.). The introduction of the QWERTY keyboard in 1873 further streamlined the writing process, preventing typebar jams and enhancing typing efficiency (Inglis, 2018). By the late 19th century, typewriters had become indispensable in offices worldwide, significantly boosting productivity (*Typewriter*, n.d.).

The transition from typewriters to electric typewriters in the 1920s marked another leap forward, with innovations like automatic correction and faster typing speeds becoming standard (*Typewriter*, n.d.). By the mid-20th century, typewriters had empowered countless writers and professionals, including many women who entered the workforce as typists, transforming gender roles and economic dynamics (*Typewriter*, n.d.). The cultural impact of typewriters has undeniably shaped business communication and literary creation for decades.

The advent of personal computers and laptops in the digital revolution further transformed the freelance writing landscape. Portable typewriters like the Corona gave way to powerful laptops, allowing writers to work from virtually anywhere. This shift enhanced convenience and enabled the integration of digital tools, making research, writing, and editing more efficient.

Why AI is Important for Writers

Artificial intelligence (AI) is a buzzword and a powerful tool that can revolutionize your freelance writing. By automating routine tasks and providing advanced writing aids, AI significantly boosts your efficiency and productivity. Tools like Grammarly and Hemingway Editor help you produce polished content quickly, reducing the time spent on editing and proofreading. Additionally, AI-driven research tools can compile relevant information in seconds, allowing you to focus more on creative aspects rather than tedious data gathering. The practical benefits of AI in freelance writing are undeniable.

Staying competitive in the freelance market requires more than just writing skills. It demands the use of new technologies. Leveraging AI tools provides a competitive advantage by boosting productivity, improving content quality, and ensuring consistency. This is crucial in maintaining client satisfaction and securing repeat business. For instance, AI-powered content generation platforms like Jasper can assist in creating high-quality content tailored to specific audiences, ensuring that you effectively meet diverse client needs.

AI enables freelance writers to manage increased workloads while upholding exceptional quality, which is vital for expanding clientele and income. The rapid evolution of AI suggests forthcoming advancements, including predictive analytics for content trends and tailored writing support. Staying ahead in the freelance writing industry necessitates ongoing learning and adaptation to emerging technologies like AI.

Embracing AI is not just about keeping up with technological advancements; it's about leveraging these tools to enhance your writing capabilities and stay ahead in a competitive market. With the transformative journey of freelance writing and the critical role of AI in mind, let's delve into an overview of the book.

Overview of the Book

The AI Freelancer: Leveraging Artificial Intelligence to Boost Your Writing Career is your essential guide to integrating AI into your freelance writing practice. This book aims to offer a thorough insight into how AI enhances productivity, efficiency, and competitiveness. It begins by exploring the evolution of freelance writing, from the early days of typewriters to the modern digital age, setting the stage for AI's transformative impact.

The book organizes its content into four main parts.

- **Getting Started with AI Tools** introduces essential AI tools that can revolutionize your writing workflow. You'll learn about AI writing assistants like Grammarly and ProWritingAid, content generation tools like Jasper and Writesonic, and research aids like Google Scholar and AI-powered data analysis tools. This section also covers project management and productivity tools to help you streamline your tasks.

- **Enhancing Writing Quality with AI** delves into improving grammar and style, generating and optimizing content, and editing and refining your work with AI-powered tools. You will discover how to leverage AI for grammar checks, style enhancements, readability improvements, and SEO optimization, ensuring your content meets the highest standards.

- **Managing Your Freelance Writing Business with AI** focuses on using AI for marketing, client acquisition, and administrative tasks. You'll explore how AI can automate social media marketing, enhance email campaigns, optimize your website, and manage client relationships effectively. This section also covers invoicing, time tracking, and document management to keep your business running smoothly.

- **Advancing Your AI Skills and Staying Ahead** provides insights into advanced AI techniques, continuous learning, and staying updated with AI innovations. You'll learn about natural language processing, machine learning, AI-driven market analysis, and writing for global audiences. Continuous skill development and networking within the AI community are emphasized in this part, highlighting their importance. This emphasis on constant learning should motivate writers to stay updated and feel more confident in adapting to new technologies.

With clear examples, practical advice, and step-by-step guidance, this book equips you to harness the power of AI, enhance your writing career, and keep you competitive in the evolving landscape of freelance writing. Now, let's explore artificial intelligence and its core concepts.

Understanding Artificial Intelligence

AI has quickly shifted from a science fiction concept to a transformative power across different industries. To maximize its potential, grasp AI's core concepts and impact on creative fields. Let's explore the basics of AI and its applications in creative industries and dispel some common misconceptions.

Defining AI and Its Core Concepts

Artificial intelligence enables machines to simulate human intelligence, allowing them to think and act like humans. Core concepts supporting AI include machine learning, neural networks, and natural language processing (NLP).

Machine Learning and Neural Networks

Machine learning (ML) focuses on constructing systems that learn from data and enhance performance over time without requiring explicit programming. Algorithms analyze patterns in data, make predictions, and adapt their operations based on feedback.

Netflix employs machine learning algorithms to recommend shows by dissecting your viewing record. These algorithms continuously learn your preferences and adjust their recommendations as you consume more content.

Neural networks get motivation from the human brain and play a crucial role in numerous machine-learning applications. These networks comprise interconnected nodes (neurons) that actively process information across layers. Each layer progressively extracts more intricate features from the input data. A well-known example is Google's AlphaGo, which used deep neural networks to defeat the world champion Go player in 2016 (*AlphaGo*, n.d.). This victory showcased the power of neural networks in tackling complex tasks.

Natural Language Processing (NLP)

NLP enables machines to comprehend, analyze, and react to human language by combining computational linguistics with machine learning to process vast amounts of natural language data.

Every day, NLP plays a part in our lives, often without our knowing. Virtual aides like Siri and Alexa utilize NLP to comprehend orders and react appropriately. Furthermore, NLP drives sentiment analysis tools that assist businesses in assessing customer opinions from social media posts. A study by Grand View Research projects that the NLP market will reach $43.3 billion by 2025, driven by the growing need for automated customer support and data analysis (Beccue & Kaul, 2019).

The Role of AI in Creative Industries

A deep understanding of the historical context and innovations that drove AI's development is crucial for grasping its current uses, as it profoundly influences creative industries like design, art, writing, and music.

Historical Context and Innovations

The relationship between AI and creativity dates back to the 1950s when pioneers like Alan Turing explored the possibility of machines exhibiting creative behavior (*Artificial*

Intelligence, n.d.). Early AI systems, such as the "Mad Libs" style text generators, laid the groundwork for more sophisticated creative tools.

AI innovations have spurred the creation of tools. One of them is DeepDream, a program that generates surreal visuals by processing images through multiple neural network layers. This has ignited interest in AI-generated art and prompted its integration into various creative fields.

Current Applications in Writing

AI's role in writing has evolved significantly, offering tools that enhance productivity and creativity. AI writing assistants like OpenAI's GPT-4o can create readable and contextually pertinent text based on users' prompts. These tools are invaluable for brainstorming, drafting, and editing content.

Heliograf, an AI system utilized by The Washington Post, automates the creation of news articles covering topics such as sports and election results. This automation enables human journalists to dedicate their efforts to more comprehensive reporting. According to a report by Deloitte, AI can boost productivity in content creation by up to 30% (Kandi et al., 2024).

AI also assists in overcoming writer's block. Tools like ShortlyAI can expand on your ideas, suggest new directions, and even complete sentences, making the writing process more efficient and enjoyable. As AI continues to advance, its applications in writing will likely expand, offering new ways to enhance creativity and streamline workflows.

Common Misconceptions about AI

Misunderstanding AI occurs despite its potential, which hinders its adoption due to myths and fears. Let's debunk some common misconceptions and address ethical considerations for responsibly using it.

Debunking Myths and Fears

One prevalent myth is that AI will replace humans in all jobs. While AI can automate repetitive tasks, it is unlikely to replace roles requiring complex decision-making, emotional intelligence, and creativity. AI enhances human capabilities, enabling individuals to concentrate on their work's more strategic and creative aspects.

AI systems aren't flawless; their usefulness hinges on the quality of the training data. Biases within this data can result in biased results, underscoring the necessity for meticulous data curation and transparent algorithms. Facial recognition systems, for instance, face scrutiny due to their elevated error rates in identifying individuals with darker skin tones, underscoring the imperative of tackling bias in AI advancement.

Ethical Considerations and Responsible Use

Developing and deploying AI requires prioritizing ethical considerations, particularly addressing data privacy, algorithmic bias, and transparency to ensure responsible use. The European Union's General Data Protection Regulation (GDPR) establishes stringent guidelines on data privacy, requiring companies to adhere to specific standards in managing user data.

AI decision-making methodologies are paramount for developing trust by ensuring transparency. Explainable AI (XAI) seeks to render AI decisions understandable to humans. This becomes particularly critical in domains such as healthcare, where AI systems aid in diagnosing diseases and suggesting treatments. Patients and doctors must understand how to generate these recommendations to facilitate informed decision-making.

Moreover, AI ethics involves considering the societal impact of AI technologies. For instance, autonomous weapons pose significant ethical dilemmas, leading to calls for international regulations to prevent their misuse.

Exploring essential AI tools for writers will provide practical insights as you delve deeper into AI. Turn the page to Chapter 1 to learn how to leverage technology to enhance your writing process and creativity.

Chapter 1: Essential AI Tools for Writers

Artificial Intelligence (AI) has transformed the writing process by providing tools that improve efficiency and quality. This chapter explores how AI writing assistants can become essential for writers, covering their features, benefits, and popular options.

AI Writing Assistants

AI writing assistants enhance writing quality by offering immediate grammar, style, tone, and readability feedback. They aid writers in creating polished and professional content with minimal effort. In this section, let's discuss the ones most writers use.

Popular AI Writing Assistants

Grammarly and ProWritingAid have their unique strengths and cater to different writing needs. Let's discuss them further.

Grammarly

Grammarly's user-friendly interface and thorough writing suggestions have made it famous. It examines grammar, punctuation, and style errors, detects tone, and enhances vocabulary. Its real-time suggestions are perfect for swiftly editing emails, social media posts, and blog articles online. With over 30 million users, Grammarly is a trusted tool for many writers and businesses (*Grammarly*, 2023).

ProWritingAid

ProWritingAid excels in delivering detailed feedback and thorough analysis for writing. It offers style suggestions, readability assessments, and author comparisons. This tool is handy for long-form content like novels and research papers. ProWritingAid's extensive reports assist writers in enhancing their writing style and structure.

Features and Benefits

Both Grammarly and ProWritingAid offer various features that can immensely improve your writing.

Grammar and Style Suggestions

Grammarly and ProWritingAid provide exhaustive grammar and style recommendations. Grammarly excels with its real-time feedback and intuitive corrections, making it ideal for swift edits. For instance, it can effortlessly identify and rectify missing articles, misplaced commas, and unclear sentences.

ProWritingAid provides comprehensive feedback on style and structure, pinpointing overused words, clichés, and repetitive phrases to refine your writing. It highlights instances of exact phrase repetition and offers alternatives, thereby enhancing the overall readability of your content.

Tone and Readability Improvements

Tone detection is crucial for ensuring your writing conveys the right message. Grammarly analyzes your text and suggests adjustments to make it sound more assertive, friendly, or confident. This feature is handy for business communications where tone can significantly impact the message's effectiveness.

ProWritingAid enhances readability by offering checks to ensure your essay is available to your intended audience. It provides scores and suggestions to simplify complex sentences and improve text flow. This feature proves particularly useful for academic or technical writing, where clarity is essential.

Cost and Accessibility

The free versions of both tools provide essential grammar and spelling reviews. Still, their premium versions differ in pricing and features. Grammarly's premium version unlocks advanced features like tone detection and plagiarism checks. In contrast, ProWritingAid's premium version provides extensive analysis and offers a one-time payment option for lifetime access.

AI writing assistants can significantly improve your writing process by offering real-time feedback and thorough analysis. Whether you're composing a brief email or a lengthy manuscript, these tools can assist you in efficiently creating high-quality content. Next, let's delve into content generation tools, another crucial category of AI tools for writers.

Content Generation Tools

Advanced AI technologies have revolutionized content production for writers and marketers, enabling the rapid and efficient creation of high-quality content. Platforms such as Jasper (formerly Jarvis) and Writesonic lead this transformation, utilizing automation to generate content effectively. Let's delve into their functionality and practical applications for writers.

Automated Content Creation Platforms

In today's digital landscape, producing high-quality content is imperative. AI-powered platforms such as Jasper and Writesonic can assist you in swiftly achieving this goal. This section will explore how these tools utilize GPT-4 technology to enhance your writing process, from generating ideas to optimizing SEO. Let's examine their features and advantages.

Jasper (formerly Jarvis)

Jasper, built on GPT-4 technology, empowers users with its robust AI content generation capabilities. It effortlessly assists in crafting marketing copy, blog articles, and product descriptions. A standout feature is its capacity to generate content ideas and outlines, streamlining the writing process. For example, when composing a blog post on sustainable living, Jasper furnishes a thorough outline, pertinent keywords, and initial paragraphs to kickstart the process. Its user-friendly interface and extensive templates ensure accessibility, catering to tech-savvy and non-tech-savvy individuals.

Writesonic

Writesonic is another AI-driven platform designed to facilitate content creation. Like Jasper, it's built on GPT-4 and excels in generating marketing copy, blog articles, and social media content. Writesonic stands out for its SEO optimization features, which help ensure your content ranks well on search engines. Writesonic can generate engaging and SEO-friendly content tailored to your target audience for social media posts promoting a new product. Its integration with Google Search ensures the content remains up-to-date and relevant.

Use Cases for Writers

AI content generation tools revolutionize writing by enhancing speed and efficiency. These tools help writers quickly produce engaging, high-quality content for various purposes, including blog posts, articles, and social media. Let's explore how AI platforms can streamline writing, saving time and effort.

Blog Posts and Articles

AI content generators like Jasper and Writesonic enable you to create well-researched and structured blog posts and articles in significantly less time than manual methods. These tools can generate drafts containing essential points and relevant statistics for topics like the latest AI technology trends. Using these platforms saves time and ensures your content is informative and data-supported, allowing you to refine and personalize it.

Social Media Content

Crafting engaging social media content is essential for keeping an active online presence—AI content creation tools such as Writesonic aid in producing compelling posts that grasp your audience's attention. Whether you're advertising a recent blog entry, disseminating industry updates, or commemorating a company's achievement, these tools can generate creative and engaging content customized to meet the distinctive requirements of each platform. For instance, Writesonic can assist in composing a captivating LinkedIn post that announces a new product launch, complete with hashtags and a call to action to stimulate engagement.

AI-powered platforms such as Jasper and Writesonic revolutionize content creation for writers by simplifying the process and enabling the production of high-quality, engaging content for social media, articles, and blogs.

Let's transition to the following critical topic: research and data analysis. This area is equally important for content creators, providing the foundation for accurate and insightful content.

Research and Data Analysis

AI tools are transforming how we conduct research and analyze data, streamlining and enhancing the process. We'll delve into influential AI tools for research and data analysis, highlighting their benefits for writers. Then, we'll discuss data analysis for writers, offering practical examples and insights on integrating data into your writing.

AI Tools for Research

When it comes to research, AI tools can be your best allies. They streamline the process, helping you find relevant information quickly and efficiently. This section covers essential AI tools to elevate your research game to a new efficiency level.

Google Scholar and Semantic Scholar

Researchers consider Google Scholar and Semantic Scholar essential tools. Google Scholar, a free available web search engine, indexes academic literature's metadata or full text across various publishing forms. Semantic Scholar, developed by the Allen Institute for AI, goes a step further by using machine learning to understand the context of papers, thus enabling researchers to find relevant research efficiently.

For instance, Semantic Scholar offers features like citation graphs and influential citations to help you quickly identify key papers in your field. This can be a game-changer when performing literature reviews, allowing you to focus on the most impactful studies without wading through less relevant material.

AI-Powered Research Assistants

AI-powered research assistants like Elicit, Litmaps, and Research Rabbit offer more tailored research support. Elicit helps you identify relevant research by allowing you to ask semantic questions rather than just keyword searches. Litmaps creates visualizations of research papers, helping you see connections between different works. Research Rabbit, dubbed "The Spotify for Research," curates personalized collections of research based on your interests, much like a music playlist (Bello, 2024).

Using tools like Research Rabbit can significantly reduce the time spent on preliminary research stages. This capability allows you to analyze and write more deeply by discovering new perspectives and connections that traditional search methods might overlook.

Data Analysis for Writers

As a writer, tapping into data analysis can elevate your content to new heights. Understanding trends and insights derived from data helps you stay relevant and engaging. Let's explore how AI tools for trend analysis and data visualization can transform your writing, making it more authoritative, informative, and impactful.

Analyzing Trends and Insights

Understanding trends and insights derived from data can benefit scientists, statisticians, and writers. Tools like Google Trends enable you to identify popular topics, empowering you to tailor your content to align with reader interests. For instance, if you observe a spike in interest in a specific subject, you can create content that capitalizes on that trend, enhancing your ability to engage your audience.

AI tools can discover correlations and patterns within extensive datasets that may take time to be evident through analysis. For instance, you can utilize an AI tool to analyze social media trends, revealing the most discussed topics and their associated sentiments. This analysis can inform your writing, effectively enabling you to address your audience's concerns and interests.

Incorporating Data into Writing

Integrating data into your writing enhances its authority and depth. Utilize data visualization tools such as Tableau and Power BI to craft compelling charts and graphs, simplifying complex data for your readers. For instance, when composing an article on climate change, employ these tools to illustrate temperature trends over the past century, strengthening your argument's persuasiveness.

AI can also assist in interpreting data. Tools like Scite provide innovative citation analysis, showing how others have cited an article and whether the citations are supportive or disputative. This context can add depth to your analysis, helping you build a more nuanced argument.

Writesonic, an AI tool, can seamlessly transform raw data into engaging narratives and meaningful insights. It can generate long-form articles integrating data-driven insights and quickly draft informative and engaging content.

Powerful capabilities offered by AI tools for research and data analysis can significantly enhance your work as a writer, saving you time, providing deeper insights, and helping you create more compelling content whether you're conducting a literature review, analyzing data trends, or incorporating data into your writing.

Now that you understand research and data analysis, the next crucial step for any writer or researcher is project management and organization. Practical project management tools can help you keep track of your progress, manage deadlines, and collaborate with others. Let's explore how AI can enhance your project management and organizational skills.

Project Management and Organization with AI

Today's fast-paced world sees AI revolutionizing project management and organization. AI significantly boosts productivity and streamlines workflows when integrated into task and time management tools such as Trello, Asana, and Notion AI. This guide will explore how AI can transform project management productivity and streamline workflows through tools like RescueTime and Focus@Will.

AI in Task Management

Efficient task administration plays a crucial role in increasing productivity. Incorporating AI into your task management tools can revolutionize your workflow, enhancing its efficiency and making it more streamlined. This section examines how AI-powered tools such as Trello, Asana, and Notion can assist in automating actions, optimizing workflows, and effortlessly managing projects.

Trello and Asana with AI Integrations

Trello and Asana, two of the most prevalent project management tools, have integrated AI to enhance task management.

Trello uses AI to automate routine actions, provide intelligent suggestions, and help you stay ahead of deadlines. Its intuitive Kanban board system allows you to organize tasks visually. For instance, Trello's AI can suggest moving cards based on past activity patterns, helping you prioritize tasks more effectively. This feature helps manage multiple projects and deadlines without manually updating each task's status.

Asana's AI-powered tools analyze project data to pinpoint bottlenecks, propose task assignments, and advise on resource allocation, enhancing team alignment and productivity. The AI predicts project outcomes and potential risks, enabling data-driven decision-making. If a project falls behind schedule, Asana can recommend reallocating resources to critical tasks to meet deadlines.

The free plans for both tools offer basic features while upgrading to Asana's premium plan, which unlocks advanced features like comprehensive status updates and competent project answers, which enhance team collaboration and efficiency.

Notion AI

Notion AI transforms into a robust project management tool by integrating AI capabilities that enhance documentation and task management. Notion AI can summarize content, brainstorm ideas, draft documents, and correct grammar. This mainly benefits content-centric workflows, such as marketing or research projects. For instance, Notion AI can generate a rough draft for a blog post based on your input, saving you valuable time during the content creation.

Notion's AI boosts productivity by reducing manual data entry and editing time through intelligent recommendations and automating repetitive tasks, thus helping manage project data more efficiently.

Time Management and Productivity Tools

To stay ahead, managing your time and boosting productivity becomes crucial. AI tools such as RescueTime and Focus@Will can make a significant difference by offering insights and optimizations tailored to your workflow, ensuring you remain focused and efficient. Let's delve into how these tools can transform your work habits.

RescueTime

RescueTime, an AI-powered tool, tracks your digital activity to provide detailed reports on how you spend your time and helps improve productivity. It enables you to identify productivity blocks and make informed decisions about time management by analyzing your tasks and website usage.

For example, if you spend too much time on social media, RescueTime can alert you and suggest more productive activities. It can also block distracting websites during work hours, helping you focus on your tasks.

Focus@Will

Focus@Will uses AI to enhance your concentration and productivity through specially designed music playlists. These playlists are tailored to your productivity style, helping you maintain focus and work more efficiently. According to research, music can significantly improve concentration and reduce stress, leading to better work performance (Heshmart, 2021).

Focus@Will's AI selects music tracks based on your feedback, continuously optimizing the playlist to keep you productive. This tool is handy for tasks that require deep concentration, such as writing or coding.

AI integration in project and time management tools can revolutionize task management and optimize productivity. Intelligent automation and predictive analytics in tools like Trello, Asana, and Notion AI streamline workflows and enhance collaboration. RescueTime and Focus@Will help individuals effectively manage their time and sustain daily focus. Leveraging these AI-powered tools can lead to greater project efficiency and productivity.

Key Takeaways

- AI has revolutionized writing with tools like Grammarly and ProWritingAid that enhance efficiency and quality.

- Grammarly provides user-friendly, real-time grammar and style suggestions, which are ideal for quick edits and online writing.

- ProWritingAid offers detailed feedback on style and structure, which is beneficial for long-form content such as novels and research papers.

- Both tools provide grammar and style suggestions, with Grammarly excelling in real-time corrections and ProWritingAid offering in-depth analysis.

- Tone detection and readability improvements are crucial features; Grammarly adjusts tone, while ProWritingAid ensures accessibility to the audience.

- AI-powered tools such as Jasper and Writesonic efficiently create high-quality content quickly.

- Jasper generates content ideas and outlines, while Writesonic excels in SEO optimization.

- Research and data analysis tools like Google Scholar, Semantic Scholar, Elicit, Litmaps, and Research Rabbit streamline the research process.

- AI tools can analyze trends and insights, helping writers tailor content to meet reader interests.

- Incorporating data into writing adds authority and depth; data visualization tools like Tableau and Power BI make complex data understandable.

- AI integrations in project management and organization tools such as Trello, Asana, and Notion enhance productivity.

- Trello automates routine actions and provides intelligent suggestions, while Asana offers workflow optimization and predictive analytics.

- Notion AI enhances documentation and task management by generating content drafts and automating tasks.

- Time management tools like RescueTime track digital activity, helping identify productivity blocks and manage time effectively.

- Focus@Will uses AI to enhance concentration and productivity through specially designed music playlists.

- Integrating AI into project and time management tools revolutionizes task management and boosts productivity through intelligent automation and predictive analytics.

Now that you understand how AI can boost your productivity, it's time to set up your AI workspace. Creating a workspace tailored to your needs is essential for maximizing efficiency. In the next chapter, we will walk through the tools and strategies for designing an AI-enhanced environment where you can work smarter and more effectively.

Chapter 2: Setting Up Your AI Workspace

Setting up your AI workspace enhances productivity and ensures a smooth workflow. It empowers you to manage your writing process effectively. This chapter will help you choose the right tools, evaluate them based on your needs and budget, and integrate them smoothly into your routine. By the end, you'll have a fully functional AI-powered workspace ready to handle any writing project and enhance your productivity and creativity.

Choosing the Right Tools

Choosing the right AI tools can make a difference in your writing process. The AI tool market offers various products with distinct features and advantages. You must match the tools to your writing goals and consider your budget to make the best choice.

Evaluating AI Tools for Your Needs

Choosing the right AI tools can transform your writing process. Evaluating your options based on your specific goals and budget ensures you get the best fit. This section will guide you through aligning tools with your writing objectives and managing costs effectively, helping you make informed decisions.

Matching Tools to Writing Goals

Let your writing goals determine the tools you select. For example, OpenAI's GPT-4, which generates human-like text, or Jasper AI, a natural language processing tool, are excellent for creating content. These tools assist in brainstorming, drafting articles, and crafting engaging narratives.

For instance, an author crafting a fantasy novel used GPT-4 to create unique character backstories and plot twists, significantly speeding up the writing process. If you aim to enhance your content's technical accuracy and readability, tools like Grammarly or ProWritingAid are more beneficial. These tools offer advanced grammar checks, style suggestions, and readability improvements, helping refine your writing and make it more fascinating for your readers.

Statistics show that writers using AI tools can increase their productivity by up to 30% (Korolov, 2024). This boost in efficiency is not just a temporary fix but a stepping stone towards continuous growth and improvement. The AI's ability to handle repetitive tasks and provide instant feedback allows you to focus on the creative aspects of writing, fostering a sense of hope and motivation for your writing journey.

Budget is another critical factor when selecting AI tools. High-end AI tools can be expensive, but plenty of affordable or free options are available. You need to evaluate the cost-benefit ratio of each tool carefully. For example, a subscription to Jasper AI might cost around $29 per month. Still, if it saves you several hours of writing and editing time each week, the investment can be well worth it.

Many AI tools provide free trials or tiered pricing options, allowing you to start with a basic version and upgrade as your requirements increase. For example, when billed annually, Grammarly presents a free version with crucial features and a paid one with cutting-edge capabilities at $11.66 monthly.

Integrating Tools into Your Workflow

Once you've chosen the right tools, the next step is integrating them into your workflow. This integration should be seamless to ensure you can maximize AI's benefits without disrupting your existing processes. However, incorporating new tools can sometimes present challenges. To overcome this, consider starting with a phased approach, gradually incorporating the tools into your workflow, and seeking support from the tool's developers or user communities if needed.

Seamless Adoption Strategies

Adopting new tools can be challenging, but it can be a smooth process with the right strategies. Begin by exploring and understanding the tool's features and functionalities. Many AI tools offer tutorials, webinars, and customer support to help you get started.

For example, when integrating Grammarly into your writing process, you can begin by using it for basic grammar checks. This lets you get familiar with the tool and its basic features without feeling overwhelmed. You can gradually use its advanced features, such as plagiarism checks and tone detection. This phased approach allows you to adapt to the tool and its capabilities, enhancing your productivity and writing quality without causing unnecessary disruptions to your workflow.

Another effective strategy is to integrate AI tools into your existing platforms. Many AI writing tools integrate directly with popular word processors like Microsoft Word and Google Docs through plugins or extensions. For instance, you can use Grammarly's plugin for Google Docs to check your writing for grammar and spelling errors directly within the document, enhancing productivity without switching between different applications.

Maximizing Compatibility

Ensuring that your AI tools work seamlessly with each other and your existing software is essential for maintaining a smooth workflow. When tools are incompatible, it can cause inefficiencies and frustration, negating the advantages of using AI.

For example, if you use Scrivener to organize your writing projects, check if your AI tools can integrate. Many AI tools offer APIs or third-party integrations to enhance compatibility. You can incorporate OpenAI's GPT-4 with various writing and productivity tools through APIs, enabling you to utilize its features across multiple platforms.

Additionally, consider the compatibility of AI tools with your operating system. Developers typically design AI tools to be compatible across multiple platforms. Still, verifying compatibility before making a purchase is always a good idea. This step ensures you can use the tools seamlessly on your preferred devices, whether working on a PC, Mac, or mobile device.

Anecdotes and Examples

Let's consider Jane, a freelance writer who struggled with productivity due to frequent distractions and a lack of structured workflow. After integrating AI tools like Trello for task management, Grammarly for editing, and Jasper AI for content generation, she noticed a significant improvement in her efficiency. Jane's output increased by 40%, and she could take on more clients, ultimately boosting her income.

Seamless Integration Tips

To ensure a seamless integration of AI tools into your workflow, follow these tips:

- **Start Small:** Begin with one or two tools, and gradually incorporate more as you build confidence and become familiar with them.

- **Use Tutorials and Training:** Take advantage of the resources provided by AI tool developers, such as tutorials, webinars, and customer support.

- **Customize Settings:** Adjust the settings of your AI tools to match your specific needs and preferences. For instance, you can customize the language style or tone of the AI-generated text, set the tool to focus on particular grammar or style rules or adjust the level of feedback or suggestions the tool provides.

- **Regular Updates:** Keep your tools current to take advantage of the latest features and refinements. Regularly updating allows you to access new functionalities, enhance the tool's performance and accuracy, and ensure compatibility with the latest operating systems or writing platforms, ultimately boosting your productivity and writing quality.

- ☐ **Seek Community Support:** Join user communities and forums to share experiences, get tips, and troubleshoot issues.

Following these tips ensures that your AI tools enhance your writing process without causing unnecessary disruptions.

Setting up your AI workspace involves choosing the right tools based on your writing goals and budget and integrating them seamlessly into your workflow. By doing so, you can leverage the power of AI to boost your productivity, enhance your writing quality, and achieve your creative goals.

With your AI workspace set up and tools integrated smoothly, the next step is to customize these tools to suit your specific needs and preferences.

Customizing Your AI Tools

Maximizing the potential of your AI tools requires customizing them effectively. You should adjust the settings to suit your specific needs and preferences. This guide will help you optimize settings for peak performance, such as fine-tuning the language style or tone of AI-generated text and creating templates and macros to improve efficiency and automate repetitive tasks.

Tailoring Settings for Optimal Performance

Unlocking your AI tool's full potential starts with tailoring settings for optimal performance. You'll personalize features to suit your unique needs and adjust for different writing styles. This ensures your AI works seamlessly with you, enhancing your productivity and elevating the quality of your work. Let's get started!

Personalization Features

Imagine you've just bought a new car. Would you start driving it without adjusting the controls, mirrors, and seats to suit your needs? Certainly not. The same principle applies to AI tools. Personalizing AI features enhances your experience, ensuring a smooth and highly productive interaction.

AI tools offer numerous personalization options. For instance, you can modify your user interface, choose your preferred language, and set notification preferences. These features go beyond aesthetics; they are crucial in optimizing your workflow.

To personalize your AI tool effectively, adjust the interface layout by placing frequently used features in easily accessible spots. This strategic arrangement reduces time spent navigating menus, saving valuable time throughout the day.

Another critical aspect is customizing your AI's behavior and responses. For instance, if you use an AI writing assistant, you can set it to mimic your writing style. This involves training the AI on samples of your work. Over time, the AI becomes more adept at generating content that matches your voice, reducing the need for extensive edits.

Adjusting for Different Writing Styles

No two writers are the same. Whether you're a journalist, novelist, or business writer, your style is unique. You can fine-tune AI tools to align with your stylistic preferences, ensuring the output consistently meets your expectations.

Imagine writing a formal business report requiring your AI tool to generate concise and professional language. On the other hand, if you're working on a creative short story, you would want the AI to use more descriptive and imaginative phrasing. Tailoring the AI settings can save you considerable time and effort.

Natural language processing (NLP) technology is essential in this context. Modern AI tools, like GPT-4, come with sophisticated NLP capabilities designed for various writing styles. When you provide the AI with examples of your preferred style, it can learn to mimic your specific tone and structure accurately.

Research supports the effectiveness of this approach. A 2023 report by OpenAI revealed that users who customized their AI's writing style saw a 40% reduction in editing time (Winn, 2023). This approach increases efficiency and improves the overall quality of the output.

Creating Templates and Macros

Creating templates and macros enhances your efficiency by streamlining workflows. Using predefined formats and automating duplicative chores saves time for more creative objectives. This approach boosts productivity and ensures your writing projects remain consistent and high-quality.

Efficiency through Predefined Formats

Templates significantly boost efficiency by providing a consistent structure for repeated use. Instead of starting from scratch, you can use these predefined formats to streamline drafting emails, reports, or presentations, making the entire process faster and more organized.

For instance, using a template for meeting agendas can save significant time. Instead of manually formatting each document, you input the details. This approach ensures your communications remain consistent and professional. Templates are precious in collaborative settings, as standardized formats streamline your team's review and approval process.

Automating Repetitive Tasks

Repetitive tasks can significantly reduce productivity. This is where macros become helpful. Macros are instructions designed to automate everyday duties, letting you focus on more complicated and creative facets of your work.

Take data entry as an example. Automating this process with a macro can save you considerable time if you often input data into spreadsheets. Rather than entering information manually, the macro completes the task with a single command, speeding up the process and minimizing the risk of errors.

Automation is not limited to data entry. You can create macros for various tasks, from formatting documents to sending automated emails. For instance, if you regularly generate reports, a macro can compile data, format the document, and distribute it to stakeholders.

Putting Things Together

Customizing your AI tools through personalization, templates, and macros can revolutionize your workflow. These strategies enhance efficiency and improve the quality of your work. Tailoring your AI tools to your specific needs unlocks their full potential.

For example, imagine you're a content creator managing multiple projects. Personalizing your AI tool to match your writing style ensures that each piece of content maintains a consistent voice. Templates for recurring tasks, like social media posts or newsletters, streamline the process and ensure uniformity. Meanwhile, automating repetitive tasks frees up your time to focus on creative aspects, like brainstorming new ideas or refining your strategy.

Customizing AI tools involves more than a standard approach. You must tailor settings, templates, and macros to fit your needs and preferences. This effort is worthwhile. You can boost productivity, enhance quality, and create a smoother workflow by fine-tuning your AI tools.

As you refine your AI tools, you'll find new ways to use their features effectively. Improving your skills is essential to stay competitive in today's fast-paced world.

Now that you've mastered customizing your AI tools, it's time to explore how these technologies can enhance your learning and development efforts.

Learning and Development in AI

In the dynamic world of freelance writing, staying ahead with AI is crucial. This guide explores top training resources, tutorials, and strategies to update you on AI advancements and help you enhance your efficiency and creativity.

Training Resources and Tutorials

Finding the right training resources and tutorials can make a significant difference in mastering AI tools. You can enhance your skills and stay updated, from online courses and webinars to community forums and support groups. Let's explore these avenues to help you grow as an AI-driven freelance writer.

Online Courses and Webinars

Learning about AI effectively involves engaging with online courses and webinars. These resources offer structured lessons and the latest insights. For example, Coursera, edX, and Udemy offer a broad spectrum of AI and machine learning classes. You can choose from beginner to advanced levels to match your skill set.

Take, for instance, Andrew Ng's *AI for Everyone* course on Coursera. This course demystifies AI concepts and explains their practical applications, making it an excellent starting point for freelance writers looking to integrate AI into their workflow. According to Coursera, over 500,000 learners have enrolled in this course, highlighting its popularity and effectiveness.

Webinars are valuable resources featuring industry experts who share their insights and experiences. For instance, AI Writing Assistants often host webinars using their tools to enhance productivity and creativity. Attending these sessions lets you acquire practical tips and insights from developers and experienced users.

Community Forums and Support Groups

Learning doesn't just happen through structured courses. Engage with community forums and support groups to further your knowledge of AI tools. Platforms like specialized AI forums, Stack Overflow, and Reddit provide spaces to inquire, share experiences, and find solutions from fellow users.

Many freelance writers share success stories about solving complex problems on these forums. For instance, a writer struggling to optimize an AI-driven content generator might discover a detailed answer on a Reddit thread, complete with examples and user feedback. These communities are vital in helping users troubleshoot issues and stay informed about the latest best practices. They provide essential support and knowledge-sharing opportunities, ensuring members can effectively navigate and adapt to evolving technologies.

Support groups on Facebook and LinkedIn provide practical insights by connecting you with AI professionals and experts. Engaging in these groups keeps you updated on the latest innovations and trends in the field through active discussions and shared knowledge.

Staying Updated with AI Advancements

To stay competitive, professionals must regularly update their skills by staying informed about industry news and trends and engaging in continuous learning. Taking a proactive approach ensures that expertise remains current and innovative. Let's explore methods for staying informed and enhancing AI skills.

Industry News and Trends

Freelance writers using AI must stay informed about industry information and trends as the AI landscape develops rapidly, with new tools, features, and discoveries arising regularly. They can do so by subscribing to industry newsletters, following key AI researchers on social media, and reading AI-related blogs and publications.

For instance, websites like AI News and TechCrunch provide daily updates on AI advancements. These sources cover everything from new AI tools to significant research findings.

Attending AI conferences and seminars provides direct insights into the latest trends. Events like the AI Summit and NeurIPS (Conference on Neural Information Processing Systems) gather leading experts in AI and showcase future technologies. By participating, even virtually, you can spark new ideas and stay updated with current advancements.

Continuous Learning Practices

Mastering AI in freelance writing requires embracing continuous learning practices. As AI evolves rapidly, you need to stay current through ongoing education. Regularly dedicating time to learning new skills and updates will help you keep pace with technological advancements.

Dedicating just one hour weekly to reading AI research papers or experimenting with new AI tools can significantly enhance your skills. Websites like arXiv and Google

Scholar offer many research papers, providing detailed insights into AI theories and practical applications, which help you understand its core mechanisms and uses.

Another effective practice is participating in AI-related challenges and competitions. Platforms like Kaggle host numerous AI and machine learning competitions, allowing you to apply your knowledge and learn from others. These competitions often involve real-world problems, offering a practical learning experience.

Embracing AI in freelance writing requires a proactive approach to learning and development. You can build a strong foundation in AI by leveraging online courses, webinars, community forums, and support groups. Staying updated with industry news and adopting continuous learning practices will ensure you remain at the forefront of AI advancements.

Next, we'll explore overcoming initial challenges when integrating AI into your freelance writing workflow.

Overcoming Initial Challenges

Embarking on the journey with AI tools in freelance writing can be thrilling yet challenging. You may encounter technical issues, resistance to adopting new workflows, and a need for more confidence. This guide aims to help you overcome these initial obstacles, ensuring a seamless integration of AI into your freelance writing arsenal.

Common Technical Issues and Fixes

Technical glitches can slow you down, but they don't have to stop you. Learn to troubleshoot fundamental problems and access support effectively. Understanding these common issues and their fixes, you can keep your workflow smooth and efficient, ensuring you stay productive and focused on your writing.

Troubleshooting Basic Problems

When you first start using AI tools, technical hiccups are inevitable. These challenges can slow your productivity, whether a software crash, connectivity issues, or unexpected output quality. Here's how to tackle some common problems:

- **Software Crashes and Bugs**

    - **Solution:** Regularly update your software to fix bugs and improve performance. AI tools frequently release updates, so ensure you check for and install them to avoid common issues.

- **Connectivity Issues**

  - **Solution:** A stable internet connection is crucial. If you face connectivity problems, reset your router or switch to a more reliable network. For better stability, choose a wired connection over Wi-Fi.

- **Inconsistent Output Quality**

  - **Solution:** Craft clear and precise prompts to achieve better results. Vague or unclear instructions often lead to subpar outputs. Dedicate time to mastering the creation of effective prompts by utilizing various online resources and tutorials.

Accessing Support and Help

Despite your best efforts, some issues may require external support. Here's how to find help:

- **Official Support Channels**

  - Most AI tools have official backing through their websites, including FAQs, user guides, and customer service. Utilize these resources to troubleshoot specific issues.

- **Community Forums**

  - Participating in forums like Reddit, Stack Overflow, or specialized AI tool communities can connect you with user-generated solutions. These platforms are essential for discovering quick fixes from users who have encountered and resolved similar issues.

- **Professional Networks**

  - Consider joining professional networks and groups on LinkedIn or Facebook. These can connect you with other freelance writers who use AI and offer you a chance to exchange tips and solutions.

Adapting to AI Workflows

Adapting to AI workflows can be demanding but highly rewarding. You'll learn to conquer resistance to change and gain confidence in using AI. By embracing these strategies, you can fully leverage AI to streamline your writing process and boost productivity.

Overcoming Resistance to Change

Adjusting to AI workflows can be a significant hurdle, especially if you're accustomed to traditional writing methods. Overcoming resistance to change involves both mindset shifts and practical strategies.

- **Understand the Benefits**

  - AI tools help you save time by automating tasks like research and drafting, letting you focus on the more creative parts of writing. Embracing these advantages can make the transition smoother.

- **Start Small**

  - Begin by integrating AI into small parts of your workflow. Use it for brainstorming or drafting initial outlines before fully relying on it for complete content pieces. Gradual integration helps you adjust without overwhelming yourself.

- **Stay Informed and Educated**

  - To stay informed, you must engage with industry news regularly, attend webinars, and enroll in online courses. These activities will update you on AI advancements and best practices, boosting your knowledge, confidence, and competence.

Building Confidence in Using AI

Building confidence in AI tools involves hands-on practice and overcoming the initial learning curve.

- **Practice and Patience**

  - Try out various AI tools and functionalities. Consistent practice will help you understand their strengths and limitations better.

- **Seek Feedback**

- Share your AI-generated content with peers or mentors and ask them for feedback. Their constructive criticism will help you identify areas for improvement and enhance your skills in using AI effectively.

- **Balance AI and Human Touch**

    - Remember, AI tools are aids, not replacements. Combine AI-generated drafts with your unique voice and style. This blend ensures the final output is both efficient and authentic.

AI greatly benefits freelance writing, boosting productivity and creativity. To integrate AI effectively into your writing routine, address technical issues, seek support, adapt to new workflows, and build your confidence. The next step is to address the broader topic of overcoming initial challenges, paving the way for a more efficient and innovative freelance writing journey.

Key Takeaways

- Setting up your AI workspace optimizes productivity and ensures a smooth workflow by choosing, evaluating, and integrating the right tools.

- Choosing AI tools should match your writing goals and budget, offering unique features and benefits.

- Writers using AI tools like GPT-4 or Jasper AI can significantly speed up creative processes and improve technical accuracy with tools like Grammarly or ProWritingAid.

- Budget considerations are crucial; many AI tools offer affordable or accessible versions, such as Grammarly's free and premium versions.

- Integrate AI tools into your workflow seamlessly by familiarizing yourself with their features and using phased adoption strategies.

- Ensuring your AI tools work well with your current software ensures a smooth workflow and increases productivity.

- Customizing AI tools involves tailoring settings for optimal performance, adjusting for different writing styles, and creating templates and macros for efficiency.

- Templates ensure consistency and save time by providing a structured format. They are instrumental in collaborative settings, where maintaining uniformity across documents is crucial.

- Adopting AI tools involves troubleshooting common technical issues, accessing support, and overcoming resistance to change.

- To excel in freelance writing with AI, you need to continuously learn and stay updated on the latest developments in the field.

- Overcoming resistance to change requires understanding AI benefits, starting small, and staying informed and educated.

- Building confidence in using AI involves practice, seeking feedback, and balancing AI-generated content with your unique voice.

With your AI tools optimized and workspace set up, it's time to refine your writing. Improving your grammar and style will make your writing more polished and captivating for readers. In the upcoming chapter, you'll discover how to use AI tools and other resources to perfect your prose and captivate your audience.

Chapter 3: Improving Grammar and Style

Mastering grammar and style is crucial for effective communication in freelance writing. With the right tools and techniques, you can enhance your writing clarity, precision, and overall impact, making your content more engaging and professional.

Grammar Checks and Corrections

In the realm of freelance writing, impeccable grammar is non-negotiable. It's the bedrock of clear communication and professionalism. Even experienced writers can make mistakes. Thankfully, with the advent of AI, improving your grammar has become a breeze. This section covers identifying common grammar mistakes, including punctuation and subject-verb agreement issues, and leveraging AI for real-time error detection and contextual suggestions, empowering you to produce error-free content.

Identifying Common Grammar Errors

Freelance writers often handle numerous assignments, deadlines, and edits simultaneously. Amidst the chaos, they can overlook common grammar errors. Recognizing these errors is the first step to fixing them.

Punctuation Mistakes

Punctuation might seem minor but can significantly change a sentence's meaning. Take, for example, the difference between "Let's eat, Mom" and "Let's eat Mom." The first one invites Mom to join for dinner, while the second one implies she is the meal.

Common Punctuation Errors:

- **Comma Splices:** Using a comma to join two independent clauses is incorrect; you should use a period or a semicolon instead.

- **Misplaced Apostrophes:** Using apostrophes for plurals (e.g., apple's instead of apples).

- **Incorrect Use of Quotation Marks:** Place periods and commas inside quotation marks.

I once edited a blog where the writer frequently misused semicolons, creating chaotic and confusing sentences. After pointing out this recurring error and explaining the correct usage, the writer's subsequent drafts were markedly more apparent.

Subject-Verb Agreement

Subject-verb agreement errors occur when the subject and verb don't match in number (singular or plural). These errors often appear in complex sentences.

Examples:

- **Incorrect:** The team are losing.

- **Correct:** The team is losing.

Statistics show that subject-verb agreement errors are among the most frequent grammar mistakes in academic and professional writing. A study by Grammarly found that subject-verb agreement errors accounted for 20% of all grammatical errors in their users' writing (Joki, 2021).

Leveraging AI for Corrections

Integrating AI into writing tools has revolutionized editing, making it more efficient and accessible for freelance writers. These tools detect errors in real-time and provide contextual suggestions, significantly reducing proofreading time and improving the overall quality of your work.

Real-Time Error Detection

AI-powered tools like Grammarly and ProWritingAid scan your text as you write, instantaneously flagging errors and offering corrections. This feature is handy for freelance writers who need to maintain high standards of accuracy and efficiency.

Example:

Imagine you're writing an article on a tight deadline. Your AI tool highlights a real-time subject-verb agreement error as you type. Instead of waiting until the end to proofread, you can correct it immediately, saving time and ensuring your draft remains polished.

Contextual Suggestions

Advanced AI tools go beyond essential error detection by offering contextual suggestions to improve your writing style. These suggestions consider the context of your sentences, making your writing flow more naturally and coherently.

Example:

You write, "She was pleased about the news." The AI tool suggests, "She was thrilled about the news," which is a more concise and vivid expression.

Improving your grammar and style is a continuous journey, but AI makes it easier and less time-consuming. You can significantly enhance the quality of your freelance writing by pinpointing common grammar mistakes and using AI for corrections. Let's focus on refining your writing style, ensuring your content is grammatically sound while captivating and engaging your readers.

Enhancing Writing Style

Enhancing your writing style ensures your content stands out in the crowded freelance writing market. You can elevate your writing by mastering your tone and voice, maintaining consistency, and adapting to different audiences. This guide will introduce you to style improvement tools like the Hemingway App and Slick Write to polish your work.

Analyzing Writing Tone and Voice

Your tone and voice form the essence of your writing. These showcase your personality and establish the mood for your readers. Grasping and honing these aspects is crucial to engaging your audience effectively.

Maintaining Consistency

Consistency in tone and voice builds trust with your readers. When your writing style remains steady, your audience knows what to expect from you, which can foster a loyal following. For instance, if you're known for a friendly and conversational tone, suddenly switching to a formal and detached style can confuse and alienate your readers.

Consider the case of famous bloggers. Many successful bloggers maintain a consistent tone throughout their posts. Take Tim Urban from Wait But Why, for example. His posts are known for their humor and in-depth analysis. This consistency defines his brand and keeps his readers coming back for more.

To maintain consistency, create a personal style guide. Outline your preferred tone, commonly used phrases, and stylistic preferences. This guide will keep you focused, especially when working on different projects.

Adapting to Different Audiences

While consistency is critical, flexibility is just as important. Adjusting your tone and voice to fit different audiences shows your versatility and adaptability, making your content more relatable and engaging. You don't need to change your style completely; tweak it to connect with your readers better. Adapting showcases your versatility and helps you attract a wider audience.

Adopt a formal and informative tone when writing a technical article for industry professionals. Use a conversational and simplified tone for general readers with little technical knowledge.

Content tailored to the audience's reading level and interests significantly improves engagement. Users are likelier to engage with and stay on a page when the content feels relevant and accessible.

Style Improvement Tools

Even experienced writers can use a bit of assistance. Tools like the Hemingway App and Slick Write enhance your writing by pinpointing areas that need improvement.

Hemingway App

The Hemingway App is an ideal tool for simplifying your writing. It points out adverbs, passive voices, and complex sentences, guiding you to write more clearly and concisely. For instance, a sentence like "The quick brown fox jumps over the lazy dog" might be marked as too complex or having too many adverbs.

Hemingway makes your writing more readable. Clear and concise writing boosts understanding and memory retention. Simplify and shorten your sentences to help readers understand your content better.

Slick Write

Slick Write is a great tool for freelance writers. It corrects grammar and spelling and provides detailed insights into your writing style. By examining your text, Slick Write highlights potential stylistic mistakes, word variety, clichés, and frequently used phrases.

For example, you frequently use certain words or phrases. In that case, Slick Write highlights these repetitions and suggests alternatives, helping you keep your content fresh and engaging. Its ability to check for structural issues also ensures your writing flows smoothly, which is crucial for maintaining reader interest.

Practical Application

You can use tools like Hemingway to enhance your blog post on the advantages of AI in freelance writing. Hemingway will point out lengthy, complex sentences you can split for better clarity. It also recommends reducing adverbs to make your writing more precise and powerful.

Next, you use Slick Write to check for repetitive phrases and stylistic issues. You find that you've used the word "AI tools" excessively. Slick Write suggests alternatives like "artificial intelligence applications" or "machine learning tools," which you incorporate to add variety to your text.

These tools ensure your writing is grammatically correct, stylistically polished, and engaging.

The Role of Feedback

Though Hemingway and Slick Write are useful, human feedback is unparalleled. Share your work with peers or mentors and seek constructive criticism to uncover insights automated tools might miss. Join writing communities or forums to exchange feedback and learn from others.

Successful freelance writers frequently emphasize the importance of feedback. Many credit their growth to constructive critiques from writing groups or mentors. This method improves your writing and allows you to view your work fresh.

Enhancing your writing style involves:

- understanding your tone and voice

- maintaining consistency

- adapting to different audiences

- leveraging style improvement tools.

Refining these elements lets you create high-quality, engaging content related to your audience.

As you continue improving your writing style, it's essential to focus on the next crucial element: readability and clarity. This ensures your message is compelling and easily understood by your audience.

Readability and Clarity

Achieving readability and clarity in your writing is crucial, especially when using AI tools in freelance writing. Explicit, readable content engages readers and effectively conveys your message. This piece will explore assessing readability scores and simplifying complex sentences to enhance your writing.

Assessing Readability Scores

Understanding and assessing readability scores is crucial for enhancing your writing's clarity. These scores provide a measurable way to gauge the ease of reading your text. People widely use the Flesch-Kincaid Grade Level and the Gunning Fog Index readability formulas.

Flesch-Kincaid Grade Level

The Flesch-Kincaid Grade Level measures the readability of English texts by calculating the average number of words per sentence and syllables per word. It then assigns a grade-level score, showing how many years of education are needed to understand the text.

For example, if your writing scores an 8.0 on the Flesch-Kincaid scale, it means someone with an eighth-grade reading level can understand it. Tools like Microsoft Word and many online readability checkers can provide this score. Aim for a grade level that matches your target audience's reading ability. For general audiences, a score between 7.0 and 8.0 is often ideal.

Consider this example: a freelance writer revised a technical blog post about AI from a Flesch-Kincaid score of 12.5 to 8.2. This change made the content accessible to a broader audience, resulting in a 25% increase in reader engagement and positive feedback.

Gunning Fog Index

The Gunning Fog Index is a valuable tool for assessing readability. It estimates how many years of formal education someone needs to understand a text on their first reading. The formula examines sentence length and identifies complex words, which are words with three or more syllables.

For instance, a Gunning Fog Index of 12 means the text suits someone with a high school education. This index helps you identify whether your writing is too complex for your intended readers. Keeping your Fog Index around eight is typically suitable for a general audience.

A practical example: a financial advisor used the Gunning Fog Index to simplify their client reports. By reducing the index from 16 to 10, clients found the reports more straightforward to understand, leading to fewer follow-up questions and increased client satisfaction.

Simplifying Complex Sentences

Simplifying complex sentences is vital to keeping your writing clear. Long, tangled sentences can confuse readers and hide your message. Here are some practical techniques to assist you in streamlining your writing.

Breaking Down Long Paragraphs

Short paragraphs make your content more digestible. Break long ones into smaller sections. Focus on one idea per paragraph to help your audience follow your view more efficiently.

Imagine you're explaining AI concepts to a non-technical audience. Instead of a dense, technical paragraph, break it down:

·**Complex Version:** AI simulates human intelligence in machines programmed to think and learn like humans. It finds applications across various fields, including healthcare, finance, and customer service, where it swiftly analyzes vast amounts of data and offers valuable insights.

- **Simplified Version:** Machines designed to think and learn like humans mimic human intelligence. People use it in various fields like healthcare, finance, and customer service, where it swiftly analyzes extensive data sets to deliver valuable insights.

The simplified version uses shorter sentences, making the content more accessible.

Using Plain Language Principles

Plain language principles encourage using clear and straightforward language, making your writing easy to understand. Here are some basic principles:

- **Use simple words:** Choose everyday language over jargon.

- **Active voice:** Write using the active voice instead of the passive voice.

- **Short sentences:** Make sentences short and direct.

- **Bullet points and lists:** Use bullet points to organize information.

For example, when describing AI capabilities, instead of saying, "The AI algorithm analyzed the data to extract valuable insights," you could say, "The AI algorithm analyzed the data and extracted valuable insights." This revision uses plain language, active voice, and concise phrasing.

Practical Application in AI-Assisted Writing

You can significantly enhance readability and clarity with AI tools like the Hemingway App or Grammarly. These tools highlight complex sentences, suggest simpler alternatives, and provide readability scores.

For instance, a freelance writer might run their draft through the Hemingway App. The app flags long, hard-to-read sentences and suggests shorter, more precise alternatives. It also assigns a readability grade level, helping writers adjust their text accordingly.

Users read web content in an "F-shaped" pattern, focusing on the first few words of sentences and skipping large blocks of text (Babich, 2023). Clear, concise writing improves comprehension and engagement.

By assessing readability scores and simplifying complex sentences, you can enhance the clarity of your writing. These strategies ensure your audience grasps your message effortlessly, whether you're crafting a blog post, a report, or an email. Next, we will explore maintaining consistency and cohesion in your writing.

Consistency and Cohesion

Consistency and cohesion are crucial for crafting explicit, engaging, and professional content, particularly when utilizing AI tools in freelance writing. They ensure smooth flow and a uniform tone and terminology in your writing. You can achieve this using consistent terminology and maintaining a cohesive narrative flow.

Maintaining Consistent Terminology

Maintaining consistent terminology is crucial for clarity and professionalism in your writing by creating and using style guides and leveraging AI tools like Writer and Word.Studio, you can ensure uniformity in your content. These strategies enable you to manage terminology effectively, enhancing communication and ensuring everyone understands each other.

Creating and Using Style Guides

Creating a style guide is one of the best methods to ensure consistent terminology. A style guide establishes rules and guidelines to ensure uniformity in writing, addressing grammar, punctuation, and the consistent use of specific terms and phrases.

For instance, Grammarly Business emphasizes the importance of having a written style guide that is easily accessible to all team members. This guide should define your brand voice, mission, values, and target audience, ensuring everyone is on the same page and maintains the same standards across all communications.

Using AI tools like Writer can further streamline this process by enforcing your terminology management efforts. Writer allows you to create a living, breathing term base that can be edited and accessed by anyone on your team. This central source of truth ensures that everyone uses the same terms correctly, avoiding confusion and improving productivity.

Glossary Tools

AI-powered glossary generators are another excellent tool for maintaining consistent terminology. These tools can automatically create glossaries that concisely define terms related to your subject or field—for example, Word.Studio offers an AI-driven glossary generator that helps writers quickly compile comprehensive glossaries for their content, making it easier to navigate complex or specialized vocabulary.

Using a glossary tool can be particularly useful when writing technical or academic papers, where precise terminology is crucial. By providing clear definitions and context-specific explanations, you can ensure that your readers understand the terms you use and that you remain consistent throughout your work.

Ensuring Cohesive Narrative Flow

Ensuring a cohesive narrative flow is crucial for creating engaging and readable content. You'll want to link your ideas seamlessly, guiding your reader smoothly from one point to the next. Let's explore how you can use transitional phrases and AI tools to enhance the flow and coherence of your writing.

Linking Ideas and Sections

Seamlessly linking your ideas and sections is essential for a cohesive narrative flow. Use transitional phrases and techniques to guide readers smoothly from one point to the next. Well-structured writing relies on logical connections and transitions to maintain a smooth and coherent narrative.

AI tools help you by suggesting suitable transitions and organizing your content logically. These tools analyze your text and recommend improvements for flow, highlighting areas needing transitions or where the narrative seems disjointed.

Transitional Phrases and Techniques

Transitional phrases are vital in maintaining cohesion in your writing. They help to connect different parts of your text, making it easier for the reader to follow your argument or story. Some common transitional phrases include "in addition," "however," "for example," and "therefore."

Effectively using these phrases can significantly improve your writing's readability and professionalism. For example, RyteUp highlights the need to maintain consistent sentence structure and use proper punctuation to enhance the flow and rhythm of your text. This involves varying sentence lengths and using parallel structure to establish a sense of order and coherence.

Practical Applications

Maintaining consistency and cohesion becomes even more critical in freelance writing, especially when using AI tools. AI tools like Grammarly and Writer can help you keep track of your style and terminology, ensuring you deliver high-quality, polished content every time.

For example, Grammarly Business can check your documents against customizable style guides, ensuring that your writing adheres to the defined rules and maintains a consistent brand voice. This can be particularly useful when working with multiple clients or on different projects, as it helps you adapt your writing to various styles and requirements without losing consistency.

Achieving consistency and cohesion in your writing involves:

- creating and using style guides

- employing glossary tools

- linking ideas and sections effectively

- using transitional phrases.

By leveraging AI tools designed to assist with these tasks, you can ensure that your freelance writing remains clear, professional, and engaging, regardless of subject or audience.

Key Takeaways

- Mastering grammar and style enhances freelance writing's clarity, precision, and impact.

- Flawless grammar is crucial for clear communication and maintaining professionalism.

- Common grammar errors include punctuation mistakes and subject-verb agreement issues.

- Understanding punctuation errors helps avoid confusion and maintain sentence clarity.

- Subject-verb agreement errors are frequent and can undermine the quality of writing.

- AI-powered tools, notably lower proofreading time and enhance accuracy.

- Advanced AI tools offer contextual suggestions to improve writing style.

- Creating and using style guides ensures consistent terminology and uniform writing.

- AI-powered glossary generators provide clear definitions and context for specialized vocabulary.

- Linking ideas and sections with transitional phrases ensures a cohesive narrative flow.

- Transitional phrases connect parts of the text, enhancing readability and professionalism.

- AI tools can suggest appropriate transitions and organize content logically.

- Consistency and cohesion are critical in freelance writing, especially with AI tools.

- Maintaining a consistent brand voice engages readers and builds trust.

Now that you've mastered grammar and style, let's dive into the heart of freelance writing: content creation and generation. Discover how to leverage AI tools to brainstorm ideas, structure your content, and produce compelling narratives that captivate your audience and drive engagement. Ready to elevate your writing?

Chapter 4: Content Creation and Generation

Discover the transformative influence of AI in content creation. By leveraging AI tools, freelance writers can revolutionize their work, making it faster, more efficient, and innovative. This chapter delves into the benefits of AI-driven content creation, from sparking fresh ideas to enhancing brainstorming techniques. Unleash the potential of AI to ensure a steady flow of engaging topics for your projects.

AI-Driven Content Ideas

Generating fresh content ideas can be one of the most challenging aspects of freelance writing. You need a steady stream of innovative topics to keep your audience engaged, and that's where AI-driven content idea tools come into play, providing a much-needed relief. These tools enable you to brainstorm efficiently, keeping your content relevant and engaging.

Idea Generation Tools

Generating fresh content ideas can be challenging. However, with AI tools like HubSpot Blog Ideas Generator and Portent's Content Idea Generator, brainstorming content ideas becomes effortless. These user-friendly tools help you brainstorm relevant, timely, and creative topics, ensuring your content stands out and engages your audience. Let's dive into how they work.

HubSpot Blog Ideas Generator

Content creators love using HubSpot's Blog Ideas Generator. It helps you brainstorm a week's worth of blog topics in seconds. You get a list of potential blog titles and ideas by inputting a few keywords related to your niche. This tool leverages AI to analyze trending topics and keywords, ensuring the suggestions remain relevant and timely.

For instance, if you're writing about AI in freelance writing, inputting keywords like "AI tools," "freelance writing," and "content creation" could yield titles such as "10 Ways AI is Revolutionizing Freelance Writing" or "How to Use AI to Boost Your Content Creation." These suggestions help you brainstorm efficiently and keep your content aligned with current trends, saving you hours of effort.

Portent's Content Idea Generator

Portent's Content Idea Generator effectively sparks creativity. Based on your keywords, it provides quirky, attention-grabbing titles. This tool is handy for breaking out of creative ruts and injecting humor or unique angles into your content.

For exa... .e, entering "AI in writing" might generate a title like "Why AI in Writing Will Make You a Better Writer." These suggestions often include elements of surprise or humor, which can make your content stand out in a crowded market.

Brainstorming Techniques

Many people think AI limits creativity, but it enhances it. This guide explores how AI can revolutionize your content creation process, from mind mapping with AI to collaborative idea sessions. Embrace these techniques to generate innovative and well-rounded ideas effortlessly.

Mind Mapping with AI Tools

Mind mapping, a classic brainstorming technique, becomes even more powerful when incorporating AI tools. Platforms like MindMeister or XMind now incorporate AI to enhance the brainstorming process. These tools let you visually organize your thoughts, link related ideas, and uncover new perspectives.

Using AI-enhanced mind mapping, you can start with a central concept like "AI in Freelance Writing" and branch out into subtopics such as "AI tools for content generation," "AI for editing and proofreading," and "AI for audience analysis." The AI can suggest connections and subtopics you might not have considered, making your brainstorming sessions more productive and creative.

For instance, if you're stuck on a subtopic like "AI for audience analysis," the AI might suggest related ideas like "using AI for market research" or "AI tools for understanding reader behavior." This broadens your perspective and helps you create comprehensive, well-rounded content.

Collaborative Idea Sessions

AI tools can also enhance collaborative brainstorming sessions. Tools like Google Docs with AI-powered suggestions or platforms like Slack integrated with AI bots can facilitate real-time idea sharing and collaboration. Based on the discussion, these tools can suggest relevant articles, data, or even entire paragraphs, ensuring your team stays on track and inspired.

Imagine you're working with a team to develop content ideas for a new blog series on AI in writing. Using Google Docs, the AI can suggest relevant research articles or statistics as you brainstorm, providing instant access to valuable resources. This speeds up the brainstorming process and ensures your ideas are well-supported and credible.

Anecdotes and Examples

To illustrate the power of AI-driven content ideas, consider the story of Jane, a freelance writer struggling to keep her blog fresh. She started using HubSpot's Blog Ideas Generator and found it incredibly helpful. By inputting keywords related to her niche, she received a list of potential blog titles that sparked her creativity. One of these suggestions, "The Future of AI in Freelance Writing," became one of her most popular posts, driving significant traffic to her site.

Similarly, a content strategist, Mark used Portent's Content Idea Generator to break out of a creative slump. The tool's quirky title suggestions inspired him to write humorous yet informative posts about AI's impact on writing. These posts captured his audience's attention and established him as a thought leader in his niche.

Research supports the effectiveness of AI in content generation. According to a report, 65% of marketers who use AI tools reported a significant increase in their content creation efficiency (*2024 AI Content*, n.d.). Additionally, a study by HubSpot found that blog posts generated with the help of AI tools had a 30% higher engagement rate than those created without AI assistance.

These statistics underscore the advantages of integrating AI into your content creation. Using AI-driven tools and techniques streamlines your workflow, enhances your creativity, and helps you produce high-quality content that resonates with your audience. As you harness the power of AI to generate content ideas, you'll find yourself more equipped to tackle the next crucial step in your writing process: Drafting and Outlining with AI.

Drafting and Outlining with AI

Embracing AI in your freelance writing can revolutionize how you approach drafting and outlining your content. From structuring your writing to generating initial drafts, AI tools offer efficiency and creativity, transforming your workflow. Let's discover the best ways to use these tools effectively.

Structuring Your Writing

Structuring your writing is crucial for creating explicit and engaging content. AI tools like Jasper, Scrivener, and Notion can streamline the process from outlining to organizing content flow. This guide will help you use these tools to write efficiently and effectively.

Creating Outlines with AI Assistance

Crafting a robust outline forms the foundation of any well-organized writing. AI tools like Jasper, Scrivener, and Notion can aid you significantly in this essential step. Imagine you're starting a blog post on the benefits of remote work. AI can analyze similar successful articles, identify common themes, and suggest a detailed outline, saving you hours of brainstorming.

For example, Jasper's content creation feature can draft an outline based on a brief input. You provide the main topic, and Jasper generates headings and subheadings that ensure your content is comprehensive and logically structured.

An anecdote from a fellow freelancer illustrates this. Sarah, a content writer, needed help with structuring her articles efficiently. Once she started using AI for outlining, she found her articles had better flow and required fewer revisions. AI's ability to generate a cohesive structure helped her focus more on content quality and less on organization.

Organizing Content Flow

After creating an outline, the next step is organizing the content flow. This ensures that your ideas transition smoothly from one section to the next. AI tools like Grammarly and ProWritingAid can analyze your draft and suggest improvements to enhance readability and coherence. For instance, if a paragraph seems out of place, these tools can flag it and suggest moving it to a more appropriate section.

Additionally, AI ensures your piece maintains a uniform tone and style. When writing for different clients with unique style guides, you can customize tools like Grammarly to follow specific guidelines, keeping your content on-brand and professionally polished.

Drafting Initial Versions

Drafting initial versions of your content can be overwhelming, but AI tools can simplify the process. By leveraging automated draft generators and enhancement tools, you can produce high-quality drafts efficiently, allowing you to focus on creativity and strategy. Let's explore how to make the most of these AI resources.

Automated Draft Generators

Once you have a solid outline, drafting the initial version of your content can be daunting. This is where automated draft generators come into play. Tools like Jasper and Copysmith can produce a rough draft based on your outline and initial inputs. For instance, these tools can churn out a preliminary draft in minutes by inputting key points and the desired tone.

Consider the example of a freelance writer named John, who needed to produce high-volume content quickly. He could generate the first draft of multiple articles by using AI draft generators. This enabled him to concentrate on refining and polishing the content instead of starting from scratch each time.

Research indicates that using AI for initial drafts can improve productivity by 37%, especially for repetitive tasks like product descriptions or listicles (Bersin, 2023). This efficiency proves essential for freelancers managing multiple projects and tight deadlines.

Enhancing Initial Drafts with AI

After generating an initial draft, enhancing it is crucial to meet quality standards. AI tools excel at this stage, too. For example, Hemingway Editor analyzes your draft for readability and suggests simplifying complex sentences and enhancing clarity. Similarly, ProWritingAid provides an in-depth analysis of grammar, style, and consistency, offering suggestions for improvement.

Another powerful tool is Sudowrite, designed to enhance creative writing. It suggests expanding ideas, rephrasing sentences, and adding more descriptive language. This can be particularly useful for narrative pieces or when trying to add more depth to your writing.

An example from my experience: I once used Hemingway Editor to refine a draft article on AI ethics. The tool highlighted several overly complex sentences, suggesting simpler alternatives. By implementing these suggestions, the article became more readable and engaging, ultimately receiving positive feedback from my client.

AI can also help you keep a consistent voice. Tools like Wordtune analyze your writing style and align new content with your established tone. This proves especially useful for large projects that need a unified tone.

Using AI for drafting and outlining revolutionizes your writing process, enhancing efficiency and structure. From creating detailed outlines to generating and strengthening drafts, these tools are invaluable in producing high-quality content quickly and effectively. Integrating AI into your workflow allows you to focus on creativity and strategy, leaving the more tedious aspects to technology. Now that you've streamlined your drafting process, let's move on to optimizing your content for SEO.

Optimizing for SEO

Mastering SEO is crucial for driving traffic to your freelance writing. By grasping SEO fundamentals and leveraging AI tools, you can broaden your content's reach and attract a larger audience. This guide will break down the core components of SEO, including keywords, on-page techniques, and how AI can enhance your optimization efforts.

Understanding SEO Basics

Grasping SEO basics is crucial for attracting traffic to your content. You can boost your site's visibility and attract the right audience by mastering keywords, search intent, and on-page SEO techniques. Here's a guide to help you master the basics and optimize your content efficiently.

Keywords and Search Intent

Keywords form the backbone of SEO, representing the terms and phrases people enter into search engines. Grasping search intent—the motivation behind a query—enables you to select the most appropriate keywords. For instance, someone searching "best AI writing tools" likely wants reviews or comparisons, whereas "buy AI writing tools" indicates a purchasing intent.

Example: Using a keyword research tool such as Google Keyword Planner or Ahrefs, you might discover that "AI writing tools 2024" has a high search volume. Including this keyword in your title, headings, and throughout your content ensures your post appears in relevant search results.

When I started freelancing, I didn't grasp the importance of keywords. My articles were well-written, but I needed more traffic. My readership increased once I began incorporating targeted keywords based on search intent.

On-Page SEO Techniques

Optimize individual pages for higher rankings and increase relevant traffic using on-page SEO techniques. Here are some fundamental methods:

- **Title Tags and Meta Descriptions:** Your title tag is the headline in search results. Make it compelling and include your primary keyword. Although it doesn't impact rankings, your meta description should still entice readers to click through to your site.

- **Header Tags (H1, H2, H3):** These tags structure your content, making it easier for search engines to understand. Place your primary keyword in the H1 tag and use related keywords in the H2 and H3 tags.

- ☐ **Content Quality:** Provide informative, engaging content that answers your reader's questions. High-quality content typically keeps readers on your page longer, positively impacting rankings.

- ☐ **Internal and External Links:** Linking to other relevant pages on your site (internal links) and reputable external sites provides additional context and resources for your readers, enhancing your site's credibility.

- ☐ **Image Optimization:** Name your files descriptively and include alt text for your images. This practice helps search engines grasp your images' content, boosting your SEO.

Example: A blog post titled "Top AI Writing Tools for Freelancers in 2024" with sections like "Best Features of AI Writing Tools" (H2) and "Comparing AI Writing Tools" (H3) is well-structured for SEO. Including links to other posts on your site about writing tips and external links to authoritative reviews boosts your post's SEO.

Using AI for SEO Optimization

Use AI for SEO optimization to improve your content's visibility and ranking significantly. By harnessing the power of tools like SurferSEO, Ahrefs, and SEMrush, you can refine your SEO strategy, analyze competitor content, and drive more traffic to your freelance writing. Let's explore how these tools can enhance your content.

SEO Content Tools (e.g., SurferSEO)

SEO tools like SurferSEO, powered by AI, can boost your optimization efforts. SurferSEO analyzes the top-ranking pages for your target keyword and provides data-driven recommendations for improving your content, including keyword density, content length, and related terms.

Example: Suppose you're writing an article on "AI writing tools for beginners." SurferSEO might suggest including sections on the benefits of AI writing tools, standard features, and a comparison of popular tools. Following these recommendations can create a more comprehensive and competitive piece.

A study by HubSpot reveals that 75% of users stop at the first page of search results (Lieberman, 2014). Tools like SurferSEO can boost your content's ranking and drive more traffic.

Analyzing Competitor Content

Analyzing what works for your competitors can offer valuable insights. Use tools like Ahrefs and SEMrush to examine competitor content, discover their top-performing keywords, and identify which content receives the most engagement.

Example: If your competitor's article on "AI writing tools" is ranking high, analyze its structure, keyword usage, and the type of content covered. You might discover they have a detailed comparison table, which you can also include to enhance your post.

I once struggled to outrank a competitor for a particular keyword. After using SEMrush to analyze their content, I noticed they had a thorough FAQ section. Adding a similar section to my article helped me surpass their ranking within a few weeks.

Grasping SEO fundamentals and using AI tools will help you optimize your content, reach a broader audience, and boost traffic to your freelance writing work. Now that you've optimized your content for SEO, let's tackle the next crucial step: editing and refining it.

Editing and Refining Content

Editing and refining your content is crucial for creating polished and professional work, especially when you're a freelance writer leveraging AI tools. This guide will walk you through using AI-powered editing tools like Ginger Software and Autocrit, as well as the final steps to prepare your content for publication, including proofreading with AI and ensuring an error-free copy.

AI-Powered Editing Tools

Editing and refining your content is crucial for freelance success. Leveraging AI-powered tools like Ginger Software and Autocrit can elevate your writing, ensuring it's polished, engaging, and error-free. These tools are your editors, helping you deliver top-notch work every time.

Ginger Software

When it comes to refining your writing, Ginger Software is a game-changer. This tool goes beyond spell-checking; it acts as your personal writing assistant. Ginger's powerful AI analyzes your text for grammar, punctuation, and stylistic issues, making it a versatile tool for any freelance writer.

Imagine you've just finished a draft for a client. You feel confident about the content but want to ensure it's error-free and flows smoothly. This is where Ginger steps in. It provides real-time corrections and suggestions, helping you catch mistakes you might have overlooked. For instance, if you often mix up "affect" and "effect," Ginger will flag it and explain the correct usage, saving you from potential embarrassment and improving your writing skills over time.

A study from Grammarly found that writers using AI-assisted tools experienced a 74% reduction in writing errors (*How to Create a Brand*, 2021). Although this study focused on Grammarly, you can anticipate similar improvements with Ginger thanks to its comprehensive correction algorithms.

Autocrit

Autocrit is a fantastic tool, especially for creative writing projects. It offers features tailored to fiction writers, such as pacing analysis, dialogue checks, and genre-specific suggestions.

Let's say you're crafting a short story for a client who specializes in horror fiction. Autocrit can analyze your manuscript for pacing, ensuring the suspense builds at the right moments. It also highlights repetitive phrases and clichés, allowing you to replace them with more original content. This boosts your story's readability and keeps your readers captivated. Autocrit's focus on style and narrative elements makes it indispensable for refining creative content.

Finalizing Content for Publication

Polishing your writing is crucial for freelance success. This guide covers AI-powered editing tools like Ginger Software and Autocrit, as well as finalizing your content for publication with AI proofreading and manual review. These strategies will help you produce professional, error-free work that impresses clients and stands out.

Proofreading with AI

Thorough proofreading should be the final step in your writing process, even after using robust editing tools. AI-powered proofreading tools, like Grammarly and ProWritingAid, are incredibly effective. They go beyond simple spell checks, examining your text for contextual errors and offering advanced stylistic suggestions.

A freelance writer has just finished a technical blog post. Running the post through an AI proofreader can help catch those last-minute errors—such as a misplaced comma or a slight inconsistency in tone—that could detract from the article's professionalism.

Ensuring Error-Free Copy

Combining AI tools with a final manual review ensures your content is entirely error-free. AI can identify most issues, but a human touch ensures the nuances and subtleties of your writing are polished.

For instance, you might use ProWritingAid to scan your document for grammatical and stylistic errors. This tool offers comprehensive reports on your writing, from overused words to sentence length variation. After making the necessary adjustments, a manual review allows you to catch any remaining issues and ensure the content meets your standards and the client's expectations.

Many freelance writers swear by this combination. One writer shared how they managed to secure a high-profile client after using AI tools and manually reviewing their content, attributing their success to the meticulous editing process. Combining AI proofreading with human editing significantly improved content clarity and professionalism.

Editing and refining your content with AI tools like Ginger Software and Autocrit can significantly enhance your writing quality. By incorporating AI-powered proofreading and ensuring an error-free copy through manual review, you provide your freelance writing is polished and professional. Embrace these tools to elevate your writing, impress your clients, and streamline your editing process.

Key Takeaways

- Polishing your writing is crucial for freelance success, leveraging AI-powered.

- AI-powered proofreading tools go beyond spell checks, offering advanced stylistic suggestions.

- Ensure error-free and polished content by combining AI tools with a final manual review.

- Using AI tools for editing and finalizing content helps produce professional, error-free work that impresses clients and stands out.

With your content creation strategies sharpened, it's time to shift gears and focus on getting your work out there. Next, we'll explore effective marketing tactics and client acquisition methods to help you reach a wider audience and secure more freelance opportunities. Let's dive into marketing and client acquisition!

Chapter 5: Marketing and Client Acquisition

Marketing and client acquisition are crucial for the success of any freelance business. Leveraging AI in your marketing efforts can streamline processes, enhance personalization, and help you attract and retain clients more effectively.

AI in Digital Marketing

AI has transformed digital marketing, providing powerful tools to automate and enhance your strategies. Learn how AI can transform your social media marketing and email campaigns, making attracting and retaining clients more straightforward.

Automating Social Media Marketing

Social media is crucial in linking with likely customers and founding your brand. AI tools can automate various aspects of social media marketing, relieving you of time-consuming tasks and enhancing your strategy.

Scheduling Tools (e.g., Buffer, Hootsuite)

Scheduling tools like Buffer and Hootsuite are game-changers for freelancers. They permit you to design and prepare your posts across various platforms, assuring your readers stay consistently engaged.

Example: Imagine you have a busy week ahead with multiple client projects. Instead of worrying about posting daily, you can schedule a week's content in advance. Buffer analyzes your audience's actions to recommend the optimal posting periods, maximizing your reach.

According to a report by Social Media Examiner, 72% of marketers use scheduling tools to manage their social media presence (*The Big List*, n.d.). This automation saves you time for other essential tasks while strengthening your online presence.

AI for Content Curation

You can share valuable content from other sources with your audience through content curation. AI tools like Curata and Scoop can help you find and share relevant content, positioning you as an industry thought leader.

For instance, freelance writer Jane used AI content curation tools like Curata and Scoop.it to supplement her original posts. She kept her audience engaged and informed by sharing relevant articles and insights from her field, which increased interaction and client inquiries. This real-world example shows how effectively you can use AI tools in freelance writing. Companies using content curation tools experience an increase in leads, highlighting the effectiveness of sharing high-quality, relevant content.

Email Marketing Automation

Email marketing remains one of the top methods of connecting with clients. AI-powered campaigns can enhance your efforts by personalizing and segmenting your messages.

AI-Driven Email Campaigns

AI tools leverage machine learning to study your audience's behavior and enhance email campaigns. They predict optimal send times, recommend subject lines, and personalize content to individual tastes. For instance, Mailchimp is a widely used email marketing platform that leverages AI to automate and enhance email campaigns. At the same time, Constant Contact is known for its AI-driven segmentation capabilities.

Example: Imagine sending a newsletter with AI-suggested subject lines that increase open rates. AI can analyze past campaigns and suggest the most effective wording, boosting engagement rates.

Personalized email subject lines boost open rates; you can scale this personalization with AI, delivering tailored content to a large audience without manual customization. This approach enhances your campaigns' effectiveness and efficiency, allowing you to reach many clients with personalized messages.

Personalization and Segmentation

AI excels at personalization and segmentation, which are crucial for delivering relevant content to your audience. AI tools like HubSpot and Salesforce segment your email list by analyzing behavior, demographics, and past interactions.

Freelance graphic designer Mark used AI-driven segmentation to target his emails more effectively. By sending personalized offers to different audience segments, he saw a 30% increase in click-through rates and a significant boost in client inquiries.

A study by Epsilon found that 80% of consumers are likelier to do business with a company that offers personalized experiences (*New Epsilon Research*, 2018). AI enables you to create these experiences, enhancing your client acquisition efforts.

Integrate AI into your digital marketing strategy to improve efficiency and usefulness. Automating social media marketing and optimizing email campaigns can attract and retain more clients while saving valuable time. Next, let's look at ways to establish a solid online presence.

Building an Online Presence

Developing a solid digital presence is necessary for freelance writers aiming to stand out in today's digital world. Optimizing your website, which often serves as the first impression for potential clients, can significantly boost your success. AI tools for website optimization and SEO can streamline this process, making your site more appealing and easier to find.

AI for Website Optimization

Optimizing your website with AI can transform your online presence. By leveraging AI for A/B testing, user analytics, and enhancing user experience, you'll make smarter, data-driven decisions. This guide will show you how to use AI tools effectively, saving time and boosting your site's performance.

A/B Testing and User Analytics

One of the most potent ways AI can optimize your website is through A/B testing and user analytics. A/B testing compares two web page versions to resolve which one functions better. AI tools can automate this process, analyzing vast amounts of data to determine which version converts more visitors into clients. AI can quickly and accurately identify your website's most compelling design elements or content, saving you time and effort in manual testing.

For example, let's say you have two versions of your homepage: one with a bright, bold design and another with a more minimalist approach. AI-driven A/B testing can show which design keeps visitors engaged longer and which leads to more inquiries. Google Optimize and Optimizely are popular tools that use AI to run these tests efficiently.

In addition to A/B testing, AI can help you understand user behavior through advanced analytics. Tools like Hotjar and Crazy Egg use AI to provide heatmaps and session recordings, showing how visitors interact with your site. This data can reveal whether users find the information they need or leave your site too quickly.

Using AI-driven analytics helped clients increase their conversion rates. By understanding what your visitors are looking for and how they navigate your site, you can make data-driven decisions that enhance user experience and drive more business.

Enhancing User Experience

Enhancing user experience (UX) is another area where AI shines. AI can personalize content and recommendations based on user behavior and preferences, providing confidence that your site is engaging and user-friendly.

For example, AI chatbots can instantly reply to visitor inquiries, enhancing the user experience. Tools like Drift and Intercom offer AI chatbots that can handle everything from answering common questions to booking appointments, freeing up your time to focus on writing.

AI can analyze user feedback to spot everyday pain points and suggest modifications. For instance, if users often mention difficulty navigating your portfolio, AI will highlight this issue so you can make the needed adjustments. Continuously refining the user experience keeps visitors on your site longer, increasing their likelihood of becoming clients.

Leveraging AI for SEO

Boosting your online presence with AI can revolutionize your freelance writing business. By leveraging AI for SEO, you'll streamline keyword research and content optimization, driving more traffic to your website. Let's explore how these tools can help you attract clients and enhance your online presence.

Keyword Research Tools

SEO is necessary to increase your website's organic traffic, and AI can significantly enhance your efforts. Effective keyword research is the foundation of any SEO technique. AI tools can pinpoint high-performing keywords faster and more accurately than conventional approaches.

SEMrush and Ahrefs use AI to scrutinize search trends, competition, and keyword difficulty. They provide keyword suggestions that are highly relevant to your niche and have a high search volume. This helps you target the terms possible customers use to discover services like yours.

For example, if you specialize in technical writing, AI tools might reveal that "technical content writer" and "software documentation specialist" are high-performing keywords in your area. Using these keywords in your website content boosts your search engine rankings and draws in more relevant traffic.

AI-Driven Content Optimization

AI-driven content optimization enhances your SEO strategy by analyzing readability, keyword density, and overall SEO effectiveness, offering suggestions for improvement.

Grammarly and Clearscope are excellent examples of AI tools that can optimize your content. Grammarly checks for grammatical errors and offers insights into readability and tone. Clearscope probes top-ranking pages for your target keywords and offers suggestions to make your content more competitive.

Websites using AI-driven content optimization tools can experience an increase in organic traffic. Producing high-quality and SEO-friendly content enhances your odds of ranking higher in search engine results pages (SERPs) and driving more traffic to your site.

AI offers powerful tools for creating an online existence. From optimizing your website through A/B testing and enhancing user experience to leveraging AI for SEO with keyword research and content optimization, these technologies can help you attract more clients and grow your freelance writing business. You'll be well-prepared for client relationship management as you refine your online presence.

Client Relationship Management

Strong client relationships are crucial for repeat business and positive referrals in the freelance writing world. Use AI-powered tools to boost your CRM strategies, streamline communication, and ensure every client feels valued. Let's explore how to maximize the potential of these tools.

AI-Powered CRM Tools

Managing client relationships means tracking interactions, understanding their needs, and ensuring you follow up promptly. AI-powered CRM tools can help you do this with ease and precision.

HubSpot CRM

HubSpot CRM is a user-friendly tool that integrates AI to help manage your client interactions. It automates data entry, tracks customer interactions, and provides insights into your client's behavior. Imagine never missing an important email because HubSpot automatically logs your communications and reminds you of crucial follow-ups.

For example, freelance writer Emily used HubSpot to manage her growing client base. Before using the CRM, she struggled to keep track of deadlines and follow-ups, often resulting in missed opportunities. After integrating HubSpot, Emily found that the tool's AI capabilities, such as predictive lead scoring and automated task reminders, helped her stay organized and proactive. She significantly increased client satisfaction, resulting in more repeat business and referrals.

Salesforce Einstein

Salesforce Einstein elevates CRM by utilizing advanced AI features. It analyzes data to offer actionable insights, predict customer behavior, and recommend optimal times to contact clients. This tool lets you understand your clients better and customize your communication strategies more effectively.

Consider freelancer Jack, who used Salesforce Einstein to manage his diverse client portfolio. The tool's AI-driven analytics helped him identify which clients would likely need his services again soon. By proactively reaching out based on Einstein's predictions, Jack secured several repeat projects, significantly boosting his income.

Enhancing Client Communication

Compelling communication lays the groundwork for every healthy client relationship. AI can help you maintain consistent, timely, personalized communication with your clients, ensuring they feel valued and heard.

AI Chatbots for Initial Contact

AI chatbots are becoming increasingly popular for initial client contact. They can manage simple questions, offer information, and even arrange meetings. This allows you to respond to potential clients quickly, even when unavailable.

For instance, freelance writer Sarah implemented an AI chatbot on her website to handle initial inquiries. Before the chatbot, she often lost potential clients because she couldn't respond immediately. The chatbot now provides instant responses, answers common questions, and schedules calls. Sarah noticed a significant increase in client conversion rates, as prospects appreciated the immediate attention and professionalism.

Automated Follow-Ups and Reminders

Staying on top of follow-ups and reminders is critical but can be time-consuming. AI tools can automate these tasks, ensuring you get all the follow-ups and clients always feel attended to.

Consider freelancer Mike, who previously tracked his follow-ups and reminders manually, often missing them and frustrating clients. By switching to an AI-powered CRM, Mike automated these tasks. The system sent personalized follow-up emails and reminders, ensuring consistent communication. His clients appreciated the timely updates, leading to higher satisfaction and more repeat business.

AI-Powered CRM Tools in Action: Research and Statistics

Research supports the effectiveness of AI-powered CRM tools in enhancing client relationship management. Companies using AI for CRM can experience an improvement in lead conversion rates. Additionally, a HubSpot study found that businesses using CRM software experienced a 29% increase in sales (Belyh, 2023).

These statistics highlight why it's crucial to integrate AI tools into your client relationship management strategy. By automating routine tasks, providing valuable insights, and ensuring timely communication, these tools allow you to focus on what you do best: delivering high-quality freelance writing services.

Implementing AI-powered CRM tools like HubSpot and Salesforce Einstein can revolutionize client relationship management. These tools help you stay organized, predict client needs, and maintain consistent communication, leading to higher client satisfaction and more repeat business.

With AI-enhanced communication strategies, such as chatbots for initial contact and automated follow-ups, you can ensure that your clients always feel valued and heard. Embracing these technologies will streamline your workflow and significantly boost your freelance writing business. As you strengthen your client relationships with these AI tools, it's time to focus on networking and community engagement.

Networking and Community Engagement

Navigating the world of AI in freelance writing can be a solo journey, but it doesn't have to be. By engaging in networking and community activities, you'll find invaluable support, insights, and opportunities to grow your skills. Here's how to immerse yourself in AI-enhanced writer communities and collaborate effectively with other AI users.

Joining AI-Enhanced Writer Communities

Engaging with AI-enhanced writer communities is a game-changer for your freelance career. You'll gain valuable insights, discover new tools, and expand your professional network by joining online platforms and social media groups and attending networking occasions and webinars. Here's how to make the most of these opportunities.

Online Forums and Social Media Groups

AI-enhanced writers find vibrant communities in online forums and social media groups. Platforms like Reddit, Facebook, and LinkedIn host numerous groups where you can share your experiences, ask questions, and stay updated on the latest trends. For instance, Reddit's r/FreelanceWriters and r/ArtificialIntelligence have active discussions on AI tools and writing techniques.

These communities provide a space for communicating leads and strategies. You might discover a new AI tool that dramatically improves your workflow or learn how others tackle common challenges. Adults find that online communities provide valuable insights and support, highlighting the value of these networks.

Consider this example: Jane, a freelance writer specializing in tech content, struggled to keep up with her workload. By joining a Facebook group dedicated to AI writers, she learned about an AI tool that helped her automate research and draft outlines, saving her hours each week. Her connections in the group also led to collaboration opportunities, expanding her client base.

Networking Events and Webinars

Attending networking events and webinars deepens your knowledge and expands your professional network. Events like the AI Writers Conference or webinars hosted by AI tool providers offer opportunities to learn from experts and interact with peers.

These events typically include presentations on cutting-edge AI developments, engaging panel discussions, and interactive Q&A sessions. For example, attending a webinar on using GPT-4 for content creation can give you practical tips that you can immediately apply to your projects. These events also offer excellent opportunities to meet potential collaborators or mentors who can guide your freelance journey.

In one case, Mark, a freelance writer, attended a webinar on AI-driven content strategies. Not only did he gain new insights, but he also connected with another attendee who was looking for a co-author for a book project. This partnership boosted his portfolio and generated a steady income for several months.

Collaborating with Other AI Users

Engaging with other AI users can transform your freelance writing career. By collaborating on projects and sharing knowledge, you'll boost your skills and productivity. Dive into joint ventures, co-author works, and tap into a network of support and expertise to elevate your writing to new heights.

Joint Projects and Co-Authoring

Collaborating with other AI users sparks innovative projects and brings fresh perspectives. Joint projects and co-authoring allow you to combine strengths and produce higher-quality work. Whether it's a blog series, an eBook, or a research paper, teaming up with others can elevate your writing.

For instance, you might partner with a fellow writer who excels in SEO while you focus on the creative aspect. This synergy can result in content that ranks well and engages readers. Collaborative projects often result in higher satisfaction and better outcomes due to diverse inputs and shared expertise.

Take the example of Sarah and Mike, two freelance writers who met in an online AI community. They decided to co-author an eBook on the impact of AI on various industries. Sarah's strength was in thorough research and technical writing, while Mike excelled in storytelling and making complex topics accessible. Together, they produced a comprehensive and engaging eBook that received positive reviews and opened new business opportunities.

Knowledge Sharing and Support

One of the most significant benefits of engaging with other AI users is the opportunity for knowledge sharing and support. Whether through formal mentoring relationships or informal advice exchanges, having a network of peers to lean on can be invaluable.

In AI-enhanced writing communities, you can share your successes and failures, learn from others' experiences, and get feedback. This exchange of knowledge can significantly accelerate your learning curve. According to a McKinsey study, companies prioritizing knowledge sharing among employees see a 20-25% increase in productivity (Chui et al., 2012).

For example, joining a support group for AI writers can provide you with practical advice on overcoming specific challenges. When Lisa, a freelance writer, faced a block in using an AI tool efficiently, she turned to her online community. A seasoned member walked her through advanced features and best practices, helping her regain confidence and productivity.

Engaging in networking and community activities can significantly enhance your freelance writing career, especially when leveraging AI. You'll improve your skills and build a robust support system by joining online forums, attending events, collaborating on projects, and sharing knowledge.

Key Takeaways

- Networking and community engagement enhance your freelance writing career by providing support and insights.

- Online forums and social media groups provide excellent opportunities to share experiences and learn about AI tools and writing techniques.

- Networking events and webinars allow you to learn from experts and work with peers.

- Collaborating on joint projects and co-authoring with other AI users can lead to higher-quality work and innovative ideas.

- Knowledge sharing and support within AI-enhanced writing communities accelerate learning and improve productivity.

- AI tools for social media scheduling, content curation, and email marketing automation save time and enhance marketing efforts.

- AI-driven website optimization, A/B testing, and user analytics improve user experience and drive business growth.

- AI tools enhance SEO, conduct keyword research, and optimize content, boosting organic traffic and elevating search engine rankings.

- AI-powered CRM tools improve client relationship management, simplify communication, and guarantee timely follow-ups.

Now that you've mastered networking and community engagement, it's time to tackle the administrative side of your freelance business. Streamlining administrative tasks with AI will help you stay organized, save time, and focus more on your creative work. Let's explore how to make your workflow more efficient.

Chapter 6: Streamlining Administrative Tasks

Mastering administrative tasks is critical to maintaining high productivity and smooth business operations. By harnessing the power of AI, you can automate and simplify these tasks, freeing up your time and reducing errors. In this chapter, we'll delve into how AI tools can revolutionize invoicing, payment management, and other processes, making your freelance journey more efficient and rewarding.

Invoicing and Payments

Managing invoices and payments can often feel tedious for freelance writers. However, it's crucial to maintain a steady cash flow and satisfy clients. Introducing AI tools can significantly reduce this burden, allowing you to focus more on your core strength: writing. Let's explore how you can efficiently leverage AI to streamline invoicing and payment processes, providing relief from these administrative tasks.

AI Tools for Invoicing

Using AI tools for invoicing saves you time and limits mistakes. QuickBooks and FreshBooks are excellent choices, designed to simplify your invoicing tasks and make the process more efficient. By highlighting these efficiency and time-saving benefits, freelance writers can feel more productive and efficient.

- **QuickBooks:** QuickBooks is a powerful tool that automates invoicing and tracks your financials in real time. With its AI-driven features, you can set up recurring invoices, track payments, and even send automatic payment reminders to clients. For example, if you have clients on a retainer, QuickBooks can automatically generate and send invoices at regular intervals. According to a survey by Intuit, QuickBooks users reported a 40% reduction in the time spent on financial management tasks (Schwarz, 2022).

- **FreshBooks:** FreshBooks offers an intuitive interface and robust AI capabilities that make invoicing a breeze. You can create and customize professional invoices quickly. A standout feature allows you to accept online payments directly through the invoice, significantly speeding up the payment process. FreshBooks users get paid twice as fast on average compared to traditional invoicing methods.

Automating Payment Reminders

Chasing late payments is a common headache for freelancers. AI tools can automate payment reminders, helping you receive timely payments and avoid awkward follow-up emails.

- **Recurring Invoices:** Schedule recurring invoices for regular customers to secure punctual billing. Utilize AI tools like QuickBooks and FreshBooks to automate invoice sending at consistent intervals, making your billing process more efficient. For example, if you have a monthly content writing contract, you can set up the invoice on the first of each month. This strategy increases your efficiency and ensures a consistent income stream.

- **Late Payment Tracking:** Tracking late payments can be a hassle, but AI tools can do it. QuickBooks and FreshBooks offer features to monitor overdue invoices and send automatic reminders. You can configure a reminder to be sent three days after an invoice's due date and schedule another follow-up a week later if the payment remains unpaid. This automated process helps maintain professionalism and ensures timely payments.

Example: Imagine you've just completed a large project for a client. You sent the invoice, but the payment didn't come through by the due date. Instead of manually tracking it, your AI invoicing tool sends a polite reminder, followed by a more urgent one if needed. This way, you can avoid the discomfort of directly asking for payment while ensuring your cash flow remains steady.

Businesses that use automated invoicing solutions experience a reduction in overdue invoices. Additionally, companies using automated payment reminders saw a 15% improvement in on-time payments (*4 Accounts Payable*, n.d.).

By leveraging AI tools like QuickBooks and FreshBooks, you can streamline your invoicing and payment processes, saving time and reducing the stress of managing your finances. Automating tasks like recurring invoices and payment reminders ensures you maintain a steady cash flow and avoid late payments, allowing you to focus more on your creative work. Now that you've streamlined your invoicing and payments, it's time to tackle another crucial aspect of freelancing: project management.

Project Management

Freelance writing is fast-paced, and managing multiple projects can be challenging—but fear not; AI is here to help. By streamlining your workflow, enhancing collaboration, and ensuring you meet your deadlines, AI can be your secret weapon in the battle for productivity. Let's dive into how AI can transform your task management and collaboration tools, keeping you on your game.

AI in Task Management

Managing multiple projects can be challenging, but AI-powered task management tools can make it a breeze. By prioritizing tasks and tracking deadlines, these tools help you stay on top of your workload, boost your productivity, and quickly meet your deadlines. Let's explore how AI can alter your job administration.

Task Prioritization

Managing multiple projects requires effective task prioritization. Tools like Trello and Asana use AI to help you prioritize urgent tasks and decide which ones can wait. By analyzing your workload and deadlines, these AI algorithms offer tailored recommendations to keep you on track and ensure timely completion.

Imagine you have three articles to write: one due tomorrow, another in three days, and the last next week. AI can evaluate the complexity and length of each task, suggesting that you start with the most urgent and challenging piece. This helps you meet deadlines and ensures you can handle last-minute work.

Using AI for task management can increase productivity, and automating task prioritization saves time and reduces the mental effort required to decide which task to tackle next.

Deadline Tracking

Keeping track of deadlines can be daunting, especially when working on multiple projects for different clients. AI can alleviate this burden by providing automated reminders and progress updates. Tools like ClickUp and Monday.com offer AI-driven deadline-tracking features that notify you of upcoming deadlines and track your progress in real-time.

For instance, if you're nearing a deadline, these tools can alert you and suggest reallocating your time from less urgent tasks. This proactive approach prevents missed deadlines and last-minute rushes, ensuring you deliver high-quality work consistently.

One freelance writer shared that after integrating AI tools into her workflow, she never missed a deadline again. The constant reminders and progress tracking kept her accountable and stress-free.

Collaboration Tools

Boosting your productivity as a freelance writer often hinges on effective collaboration. With AI-powered tools like Slack and Microsoft Teams, you can streamline communication, automate routine tasks, and ensure seamless project management. These platforms use AI to boost efficiency, helping you stay organized and quickly meet deadlines. See how these tools can transform your workflow and bring your productivity to the next tier.

Slack

Effective communication is vital for any freelance project, and Slack is a game-changer. Slack integrates AI to enhance your collaborative efforts, making communicating with clients and team members easier. AI-powered features in Slack can suggest relevant channels, prioritize essential messages, and even automate routine tasks like scheduling meetings.

For example, Slack's AI can recognize when you're discussing a project deadline and automatically create a reminder or calendar event. Integrating AI reduces miscommunication and ensures everyone remains aligned and informed.

According to a survey, teams using Slack report a 32% increase in productivity (Virgillito, 2022). Slack's AI-driven functionalities save time and enhance the overall efficiency of communication within freelance projects.

Microsoft Teams

Microsoft Teams leverages AI to boost project management efficiency, making it a powerful collaboration tool. With AI capabilities like meeting transcription, task assignment, and document sharing, Teams facilitate smooth collaboration.

Imagine you're participating in a virtual meeting to discuss a new project. AI in Microsoft Teams can transcribe the conversation, highlight key points, and automatically assign tasks based on the discussion. This approach saves time and ensures you notice every crucial detail.

A freelance writing team used Microsoft Teams to manage a large project involving multiple writers and editors. The AI features helped them stay organized, track progress, and meet tight deadlines, resulting in successful project delivery.

Adding AI to your project management toolkit can boost your efficiency and productivity as a freelance writer. From task prioritization and deadline tracking to leveraging collaboration tools like Slack and Microsoft Teams, AI provides invaluable support in managing your workload and ensuring timely deliveries. Next, let's explore how to enhance your productivity with effective time tracking and tools.

Time Tracking and Productivity

Managing your time is a cornerstone of productivity, especially in freelance writing. Tracking your work hours and minimizing distractions is essential to maintaining high efficiency and achieving your goals. Let's explore some strategies and tools to keep you performing at your best.

Monitoring Work Hours

Effectively monitoring your work hours is crucial for maximizing productivity and accurately billing clients. Tools like Toggl, Harvest, and Clockify can provide valuable insights into your work patterns by tracking your time effectively. Analyzing this data lets you optimize your workflow, allocate your time efficiently, and improve productivity.

Time Tracking Software

Freelancing offers a great deal of flexibility, but it can also lead to inconsistent work patterns. Time-tracking software like Clockify, Harvest, and Toggl is essential for workflow management. Use these tools to monitor the time consumed on varied jobs and projects. By recording your hours, you can pinpoint tasks taking longer than anticipated and adjust your schedule accordingly.

For instance, Toggl's intuitive interface lets you start and stop timers with a click, making tracking your work in real-time easy. This insight is crucial for optimizing your workflow and dedicating enough time to each client.

Productivity Analysis

Once you've tracked your hours, analyze the data using your time-tracking software's reporting features. Generate reports to break down your project, client, or task activities. This analysis provides valuable insights into your productivity patterns, helping you pinpoint bottlenecks and areas for improvement.

For example, if you notice that you need to spend more time on research and more on writing, you can adjust your approach. According to a RescueTime report, the average knowledge worker dedicates about 3 hours daily to productive tasks (MacKay, 2019). The remaining time often gets disrupted by various distractions, leading to fragmented work patterns. You can strive to beat these averages and maximize your productive hours by analyzing your data.

Reducing Distractions

Staying focused while working from home can be challenging, but using the right tools and techniques can make a huge difference. This section explores how to focus tools like Freedom and Forest, the Pomodoro Technique, and AI-driven productivity apps can help you boost productivity and minimize distractions.

Focus Tools and Techniques

Distractions are productivity's worst enemy, especially in a home office setting. Implementing focus tools and techniques can significantly boost your concentration. Apps like Freedom, which blocks distracting websites, and Forest, which gamifies staying focused, are excellent for maintaining your attention on the task at hand.

The Pomodoro Technique, where you work for 25 minutes followed by a 5-minute break, effectively boosts focus and prevents burnout. A study by the DeskTime found that the most productive employees work for 112 minutes and then rest for 26 minutes, highlighting the importance of a balanced work-rest cycle (Gifford, 2021).

AI-Driven Productivity Apps

AI-driven productivity apps are revolutionizing how we manage our time and tasks. Tools like Trello and Asana now incorporate AI features that help prioritize tasks, set deadlines, and suggest optimal work times based on your habits.

For instance, Trello's Butler AI can automate repetitive tasks like moving cards between lists or setting due dates. This saves time and reduces the cognitive load of managing your projects. Asana's AI features can increase task completion rates, demonstrating the efficiency gains that AI can bring.

In addition to task management, AI tools like Grammarly can enhance writing efficiency by providing real-time grammar and style suggestions. This improves the quality of your work and speeds up the editing process, allowing you to deliver polished content faster.

Integrating these AI tools into your workflow allows you to streamline your processes, reduce administrative tasks, and save more time for your creative projects. As a freelance writer, leveraging AI for productivity can significantly enhance your output and help you quickly meet tight deadlines.

Tracking your time and managing productivity is crucial for success in freelance writing. Use practical tools and techniques to monitor work hours, analyze productivity, and minimize distractions. This approach keeps you focused, helps you meet deadlines, and allows you to achieve your goals efficiently. Next, we'll look into streamlining your workflow through effective document management.

Document Management

Managing digital files is essential for any freelance writer using AI tools. Effective document management ensures quick access to your work, seamless collaboration, and organized records of all versions. This guide explores critical strategies and tools for organizing digital files, leveraging cloud storage solutions, using document collaboration platforms, maintaining version control, and implementing automated backup systems.

Organizing Digital Files

When you organize your digital files effectively, you boost your productivity. An orderly file system helps you find documents fast and lowers the threat of losing vital information. Here's how you can do it:

Cloud Storage Solutions

For freelance writers, cloud storage solutions such as OneDrive, Dropbox, and Google Drive are indispensable. These platforms offer secure and accessible document storage, allowing you to access your work from any device, anywhere. For instance, Google Drive provides 15 GB of free storage. It integrates seamlessly with Google Docs and Sheets, facilitating easy storage and editing of writing projects. Moreover, these services feature robust security measures to safeguard your documents from unauthorized access.

Document Collaboration Platforms

Document collaboration platforms like Microsoft Teams, Slack, and Notion enhance teamwork by providing real-time collaboration features. These platforms allow numerous users to work together on the same file simultaneously, permitting the swift incorporation of feedback and edits. For example, Microsoft Teams integrates with OneDrive and SharePoint, allowing for seamless document sharing and co-authoring.

Version Control and Backup

Maintaining different versions of your documents and having a reliable backup system is crucial to prevent data loss and manage revisions effectively.

Maintaining Document Versions

Version control is essential for tracking changes and managing multiple drafts. Tools like Git, primarily used for software development, are also excellent for document versioning. With Git, you can monitor changes, return to earlier versions, and work together with others while ensuring no modifications are lost.

In freelance writing, version control ensures you can easily manage client feedback and revisions. For instance, using Google Docs' version history feature, you can view and restore earlier versions of your document, making it easy to compare changes and keep track of progress.

Automated Backup Systems

Automated backup systems protect you from data loss by securely storing your files in the cloud. Services like Backblaze, Carbonite, and Acronis perform computerized backups, running in the background to save your documents regularly. This guarantees that the latest versions of your files are always safely stored without needing manual effort.

Research indicates that automated backup systems significantly reduce the risk of data loss. A 2022 Cybersecurity Ventures report predicts that data breaches will cost $10.5 trillion annually globally by 2025, underscoring the critical need for solid backup solutions (*Cybersecurity Research*, 2024).

Practical Implementation

Integrating these tools and practices into your workflow can seem daunting, but the benefits outweigh the initial effort. Here's a practical approach to get started:

- **Choose a Cloud Storage Solution:** Select a platform that fits your needs. Google Drive is excellent for those who frequently use Google's suite of tools. Dropbox stands out for its reliability and ease of use.

- **Set Up a Collaboration Platform:** Establish a collaboration platform if you work with a team or clients. Microsoft Teams and Slack shine in offering real-time communication and efficient document sharing.

- **Implement Version Control:** Start using a version control system like Git or leverage the version history features in cloud storage solutions.

- **Automate Your Backups:** Invest in an automated backup service. Set up regular backups and make sure to include your most important documents.

Effective document management forms the foundation of successful freelance writing, particularly when incorporating AI tools. By organizing your digital files with cloud storage solutions, collaborating efficiently on document platforms, maintaining meticulous version control, and implementing automated backup systems, you can enhance your productivity and safeguard your work against potential data loss. Adopt

these methods to streamline your workflow and concentrate on your core strength –
writing.

Key Takeaways

- Organizing your digital files is critical to boosting productivity. Store your files securely and access them easily using cloud storage solutions.

- Cloud storage integrates well with tools, providing a seamless workflow for storing and editing projects.

- Document collaboration platforms enable real-time collaboration, enhancing teamwork and efficiency.

- With version control tools, you can track changes, manage drafts efficiently, and collaborate seamlessly, ensuring no modifications are lost.

- Automated backup systems prevent data loss by regularly backing up documents in the cloud.

- Integrate cloud storage solutions, set up collaboration platforms, implement version control, and automate backups to enhance productivity and safeguard work.

- Effective document management with AI tools ensures quick access, seamless collaboration, and organized records, boosting productivity and minimizing data loss risks.

Now that you've mastered streamlining your administrative tasks, it's time to elevate your writing game. In the next chapter, we'll explore advanced AI techniques for writers, showing you how to harness the full potential of AI to enhance creativity, improve quality, and boost productivity in your freelance writing career.

Chapter 7: Advanced AI Techniques for Writers

As a freelance writer, advanced AI techniques can revolutionize your workflow and improve your content. With tools like natural language processing and machine learning, you can create high-quality, engaging content more efficiently than ever.

Natural Language Processing

Natural Language Processing (NLP) transforms how machines understand and generate human language, making your writing more impactful. Leveraging advanced tools like GPT-4o and sentiment analysis can enhance your content, connect better with your audience, and streamline your writing process quickly and precisely.

Understanding NLP Basics

NLP empowers machines to comprehend, analyze, and generate human language. By utilizing NLP, you can improve your writing with tools that capture language nuances, making your content more effective and precise.

Language Models

Language models like GPT-4o lead the way in NLP advancements. Created by OpenAI, GPT-4o is one of the most sophisticated language models. It can produce human-like text from given prompts, offering a powerful resource for freelance writers. For instance, if you're stuck on how to start an article, you can input a topic into GPT-4o, and it will provide you with several opening paragraphs. This capability saves time and sparks creativity, helping you overcome writer's block.

GPT-4o can generate text almost indiscernible from human-written content. Deep learning algorithms, trained on diverse datasets, enable GPT-4o to understand context, tone, and nuance, achieving high sophistication. For freelance writers, this means having a versatile assistant who can adapt to different writing styles and topics.

Sentiment Analysis

Sentiment analysis is another critical aspect of NLP that helps you gauge the emotional tone of your content. By analyzing text to determine whether it conveys positive, negative, or neutral sentiments, you can tailor your writing to better connect with your audience. For example, suppose you're writing a marketing piece. In that case, sentiment analysis can ensure your message resonates positively with readers, increasing engagement and conversion rates.

Tools like VADER (Valence Aware Dictionary and sEntiment Reasoner) can perforsentiment analysis on short texts and provide insights into how your content might be perceived. Incorporating sentiment analysis into your writing process helps you fine-tune your tone and make your content more engaging for your target audience.

Applying NLP in Writing

Harnessing NLP can revolutionize your writing process, making content generation and summarization more efficient and effective. By leveraging AI-powered tools, you can swiftly create high-quality content and condense extensive information into concise summaries. Let's explore how NLP can enhance your freelance writing with practical examples and tools.

NLP in Content Generation

Content generation is one of the most practical applications of NLP for freelance writers. NLP-powered tools efficiently help you create written content, such as blog posts and articles. For instance, AI-based platforms like Jasper and Copy.ai use NLP to generate high-quality content on various topics. These tools analyze the input keywords or phrases you provide and create coherent and contextually relevant text.

For example, you need to create blog posts focused on digital marketing. By inputting key phrases such as "SEO strategies" and "social media marketing," these tools can produce drafts that you can refine and personalize. This approach speeds up the writing process and ensures you cover all essential points, providing a solid foundation for your work.

Text Summarization

Text summarization is another powerful feature of NLP that can enhance your writing process. Summarization tools help condense lengthy articles or documents into summaries, highlighting the main points and key takeaways. This is especially useful for quickly sifting through extensive volumes of data during research.

Tools like SummarizeBot and SMMRY use advanced algorithms to extract the most relevant information from a text. For example, suppose you're researching a complex topic like blockchain technology. In that case, these tools can summarize lengthy whitepapers, allowing you to grasp the essential concepts without spending hours reading.

Text summarization is also valuable for creating executive summaries, abstracts, and email communications. By breaking down information into essential parts, you can communicate your thoughts more distinctly and effectively.

Practical Examples and Benefits

Using AI tools for multilingual writing can transform how you create and share content globally. You'll learn about top translation services like Google Translate and DeepL and how to write for international audiences with cultural sensitivity and localized content. Enhance your freelance writing efficiency, creativity, and audience engagement, all while staying competitive in the market.

Enhancing Efficiency and Creativity

Using NLP tools in your writing workflow can significantly enhance efficiency and creativity. Use AI-generated content as a foundation so you can concentrate on improving and customizing the text to fit your needs. This approach speeds up the writing process and frees up mental resources, enabling you to think more creatively about presenting your ideas.

Improving Audience Engagement

NLP can also improve audience engagement by helping you tailor your content to resonate with your readers. Sentiment analysis ensures an appropriate tone, while text summarization tools help you present information clearly and concisely. You can use these technologies to produce informative and engaging content for your readers.

Staying Competitive in the Freelance Market

In the competitive world of freelance writing, staying updated with the latest AI technologies gives you a significant edge. Clients increasingly expect writers to deliver high-quality content quickly, and NLP tools can help you meet these demands. Integrating NLP into your workflow boosts content quality. It speeds up production, making you more appealing to clients and helping you land more projects.

Real-World Applications

Consider Sarah, a freelance writer specializing in tech blogs. By using GPT-4o, she cut her research and drafting time in half. Sarah inputs her topics and receives well-structured drafts, which she then refines. She boosted her productivity, attracted more customers, and greatly expanded her income.

Another example is John, who writes for an online magazine. John uses sentiment analysis to ensure his articles maintain a positive tone, which has resulted in higher reader engagement and positive feedback. By leveraging NLP, John has become one of the magazine's top writers, known for engaging and well-received content.

Understanding and applying NLP in your writing can revolutionize your freelance career. From generating content to summarizing text and analyzing sentiment, NLP tools offer numerous benefits that enhance efficiency, creativity, and audience engagement. Leverage these advanced AI techniques to improve content quality and maintain a competitive edge in the constantly evolving freelance market. Next, let's explore how Machine Learning can further enhance your writing capabilities.

Machine Learning for Writers

Machine learning is transforming various industries, including freelance writing. By leveraging machine learning, you can streamline your writing process, enhance content personalization, and anticipate trends. This guide will cover the basics of machine learning and its practical applications specifically designed for freelance writers.

Fundamentals of Machine Learning

Grasping the fundamentals of machine learning is essential to fully harnessing its potential. This section covers the core concepts, focusing on supervised and unsupervised learning and critical algorithms.

Supervised and Unsupervised Learning

People usually divide machine learning into two main types: supervised and unsupervised.

Supervised learning trains a model using a dataset with labeled examples. In this process, the algorithm learns from input-output pairs, making it suitable for tasks like classification and regression. For instance, if you're training a model to identify spam emails, you'd provide a dataset containing labeled examples of spam and non-spam emails.

Supervised learning can help improve grammar and style in freelance writing. Tools like Grammarly use supervised learning to detect and correct grammatical errors. These tools learn to identify common mistakes and suggest improvements by analyzing vast amounts of text data, enhancing your writing quality.

Unsupervised Learning involves working with unlabeled information. The algorithm identifies patterns and associations within the data without depending on predefined tags. Clustering and association are standard techniques used in unsupervised learning. For example, grouping similar articles based on their content can help you organize your work and discover related topics.

Unsupervised learning can also assist in content curation. By analyzing your past articles, the algorithm can suggest themes and topics you might be interested in writing about, saving you time and effort in brainstorming.

Key Algorithms

Several vital algorithms are pivotal in machine learning. Here are a few essential ones relevant to freelance writing:

- **Linear Regression** is used for predictive analysis. It helps you understand relationships between variables. For example, you can predict the engagement level of your articles based on factors like length, keywords, and posting time.

- **Decision trees** are great for classification tasks. They allow you to segment your audience based on their reading preferences, helping you tailor your content more effectively.

- **K-Means Clustering** uses an unsupervised learning approach to classify information into clusters. It can help you identify common themes in your writing, enabling you to create more cohesive and targeted content.

- **NLP** algorithms are particularly relevant for writers. NLP encompasses a range of techniques to analyze and generate human language. Tools like OpenAI's GPT-4o use NLP to assist with content generation, helping you craft articles more efficiently.

Practical Applications

Machine learning offers numerous practical applications that can enhance your freelance writing career. This section delves into utilizing machine learning for personalization, creating recommendation systems, and conducting predictive analytics.

Personalization and Recommendation Systems

Personalization is critical to engaging your audience. Machine learning can study how readers behave and what they like, enabling you to adjust your content to match their interests.

Recommendation Systems use algorithms to suggest content based on user behavior. Platforms like Netflix and Amazon utilize these systems to suggest films and products to consumers. Similarly, you can use recommendation systems to recommend articles to your readers, increasing engagement and retention.

For instance, if you have a blog, you can implement a recommendation engine that suggests related articles based on what the reader is currently viewing. This approach keeps readers engaged on your site longer and motivates them to explore more of your content.

Moreover, machine learning can personalize email newsletters. By analyzing subscriber behavior, you can send targeted emails with content that matches their interests, improving open rates and engagement. For example, if a subscriber frequently reads articles about AI, your newsletter can highlight similar topics.

Predictive Analytics

Predictive analytics involves using historical data to predict future events. In freelance writing, this approach helps you anticipate trends and tailor your content strategy effectively.

Trend Analysis is a typical application of predictive analytics. You can spot emerging trends in your niche by examining data from social media, search engines, and various other sources. For example, predictive analytics can help you spot upcoming topics like new software releases or tech innovations if you're writing about technology.

Predictive analytics can also optimize your content calendar. Knowing your audience's peak activity times, you can organize your posts for the most potent effect. Use tools like Google Analytics to acquire insights into user conduct and make data-driven conclusions.

Additionally, predictive analytics can improve your marketing efforts. By reviewing the performance of previous campaigns, you can forecast which strategies will be the most effective moving forward. For instance, you can use similar headlines in future articles if a particular headline gets more clicks.

Bringing It All Together

Integrating machine learning into your freelance writing practice might seem intimidating, but it's manageable. Many tools and platforms offer machine learning capabilities without requiring advanced technical knowledge.

MarketMuse employs machine learning to analyze your content and recommend specific improvements, optimizing your work for better performance. These tools evaluate keyword usage, readability, and SEO, helping you create high-quality articles that rank well in search engines.

AI writing assistants like OpenAI's ChatGPT can help generate content ideas, draft articles, and even provide real-time feedback on your writing. Utilize these tools to streamline your writing process, allowing you to concentrate on crafting captivating content.

Consider the story of Jane, a freelance writer who struggled to keep up with industry trends. She automated her trend analysis and content optimization processes using machine learning tools. This allowed her to focus on writing high-quality articles, ultimately increasing her client base and revenue.

Or think about John, who implemented a recommendation system on his blog. By suggesting related articles to his readers, he increased the average time spent on his site and boosted his ad revenue.

Companies using AI and machine learning can experience an increase in productivity. Tools like Grammarly and Hemingway have millions of users in the writing industry, highlighting the growing reliance on machine learning for writing improvement.

Additionally, 53.8% of marketers view AI and machine learning as essential for success in the next five years (Kasumovic, 2024). This indicates a significant shift towards adopting these technologies in content creation and marketing.

Machine learning offers powerful tools and techniques that can transform your freelance writing career. By understanding the fundamentals and practical applications, you can enhance your writing process, engage your audience more effectively, and stay ahead of trends. Embrace machine learning, and you'll find new opportunities to elevate your craft and grow your business. Next, you'll explore how AI-driven market analysis can further refine your freelance writing strategy.

AI-Driven Market Analysis

AI has revolutionized many aspects of freelance writing, and market analysis is no exception. By leveraging AI, freelance writers can gain insights into market trends, understand niche audiences, and customize content strategies more effectively. This transformation is compelling in a field where understanding and anticipating market shifts can significantly enhance a writer's relevance and success.

Understanding Market Trends

Grasping market trends is vital for staying ahead in your industry. AI enables you to efficiently analyze industry data, providing real-time insights and predictive market forecasts. You can fine-tune your strategies using AI's capabilities, enhance audience engagement, and accurately predict market demands.

Analyzing Industry Data

AI's ability to process vast amounts of data swiftly and accurately is a game-changer in market analysis. Traditional data collection and processing methods are labor-intensive and prone to errors, often leading to delays and outdated insights. AI-driven analytics, however, streamline these tasks, enabling you to collect and analyze data more efficiently and effectively.

AI algorithms can analyze large datasets, including social media interactions, online reviews, and various marketing data sources, to deliver real-time consumer sentiment and behavior insights. This capability allows you to identify emerging trends and understand customer preferences, optimizing your content strategies to engage your audience better.

Predictive Market Insights

Predictive analytics is another area where AI shines. By leveraging historical data, AI can accurately predict future market trends. AI-based demand forecasting models can predict product demand by studying sales information, market movements, and outward elements such as weather patterns. This foresight helps businesses and freelance writers anticipate market needs and tailor their strategies accordingly.

An example is how consumer electronics companies use AI to balance product demand and optimize inventory levels. This predictive capability helps manage resources more efficiently and ensures that the content produced is timely and relevant.

Targeting Niche Audiences

Effectively targeting niche audiences starts with understanding their interests and needs. AI tools can help you identify high-demand topics and customize content strategies to resonate with your audience. You can produce content that entertains and intrigues by leveraging data from search trends, social media, and online behavior.

Identifying High-Demand Topics

Effectively targeting niche audiences begins with identifying what they care about most. AI can analyze search trends, social media discussions, and online behavior to pinpoint high-demand topics. This approach uses data to ensure your content aligns with your audience's interests and needs, increasing the likelihood of engagement and resonance.

For instance, AI-powered social media listening tools can monitor real-time conversations on various platforms, identifying trending topics and tracking brand mentions. When you understand what your niche audience discusses, you can create content directly addressing their concerns and interests.

Customizing Content Strategies

Once you've identified high-demand topics, the next step is to customize your content strategy to cater to these interests. AI-driven tools empower you to personalize content by scrutinizing audience demographics, manners, and choices. This enables you to create messages that are not only appropriate but also specifically targeted.

For example, chatbots and virtual assistants can gather data through interactive surveys and customer engagements, providing insights into consumer preferences. You can leverage this data to craft content techniques that directly address your audience's requirements and wishes.

Real-World Applications and Benefits

The practical benefits of AI-driven market analysis are vast. For instance, a freelance writer using AI tools can quickly gather and analyze data from multiple sources, saving time and enhancing productivity. AI aids you in segmenting your audience and tailoring content, which boosts engagement rates and improves client satisfaction.

Consider the case of a new healthy snack brand using AI to analyze consumer feedback and market trends. By leveraging AI-driven data extraction and sentiment analysis, the brand can quickly identify key themes and adjust its marketing strategy to better align with consumer preferences. This strengthens the brand's market position and ensures its content connects with its target audience.

AI-driven market analysis offers freelance writers powerful tools to understand market trends, target niche audiences, and customize content strategies effectively. By utilizing AI's potential, you can gather essential insights, refine your content, and stay ahead of market trends. This boosts your writing business and ensures you consistently deliver relevant and captivating content to your audience. As we transition to the next topic, we will explore how AI can assist in multilingual writing, opening up even more opportunities in the global market.

Key Takeaways

- AI tools enable freelance writers to overcome language obstacles and enthrall an international audience.

- By leveraging Natural Language Processing (NLP), writers can enhance their work as machines can comprehend, decipher, and generate human language.

- Language models produce human-like text, helping writers tackle writer's block and boost creativity.

- Sentiment analysis tools analyze the emotional tone of content, helping writers tailor their messages to connect better with their audience.

- NLP tools assist in content generation, allowing writers to create drafts based on input keywords or phrases.

- Text summarization tools condense long documents into concise summaries, saving time during research.

- Machine learning can enhance writing by improving content personalization, predicting trends, and optimizing content strategies.

- ·Supervised learning helps improve grammar and style, while unsupervised learning assists in content curation.

- Algorithms aid in predictive analysis and audience segmentation.

- Personalization and recommendation systems increase audience engagement by suggesting content based on reader behavior.

- Predictive analytics help writers anticipate trends and optimize their content calendar.

- AI-driven market analysis enables writers to understand market trends, identify high-demand topics, and customize content strategies.

- Real-time data analysis from AI tools can save time, enhance productivity, and improve client satisfaction.

- By leveraging AI and machine learning, freelance writers can stay competitive, create high-quality content more efficiently, and better engage their audience.

Staying ahead of the curve is crucial now that you've explored the exciting ways AI can enhance your writing. In the next chapter, you'll learn how to keep up with the latest AI innovations, ensuring you remain at the forefront of the ever-evolving freelance writing landscape.

Chapter 8: Keeping Up with AI Innovations

Staying ahead in the fast-paced world of AI means continuously learning and staying updated with the latest trends. As a freelance writer using AI, it's essential to keep your skills sharp and your knowledge current to leverage the full potential of AI tools.

Continuous Learning and Development

The rapid evolution of artificial intelligence requires you to commit to constant learning and growth. As a freelance writer, this mindset enhances your writing capabilities and ensures you remain competitive in an ever-changing industry. The benefits of continual learning and development in AI are manifold, from improving your writing efficiency to enhancing the quality and relevance of your work.

Staying Updated with AI Trends

Staying ahead in the freelance writing game means keeping up with AI trends. By following reputable news sources and diving into industry reports, you can integrate the latest advancements into your work, boosting your efficiency and content quality. This empowerment allows you to take control of your writing career and feel confident in adapting to the changing landscape. You can stay knowledgeable and ahead of the curve by following these steps.

AI News Sources

To stay informed about AI advancements, regularly follow reputable AI news sources—websites like MIT Technology Review, AI News, and Wired offer comprehensive coverage of the latest developments. Subscribing to newsletters from these sources can provide daily or weekly updates directly to your inbox, making it easier to keep up with the fast pace of AI innovation.

For example, you might read about a new natural language processing (NLP) algorithm that significantly improves the accuracy of AI-generated text. Using these advancements can improve both the quality and applicability of your content. Staying updated with technological trends can increase your efficiency and productivity.

Industry Reports and Journals

In addition to news sources, industry reports and academic journals provide in-depth analyses and forecasts that are invaluable for understanding AI's broader impact. Reports from institutions like McKinsey, Deloitte, and the World Economic Forum offer insights into future trends and how they might affect various industries, including freelance writing.

For instance, a report by McKinsey might predict the rise of AI tools capable of creating highly personalized content, which you could use to tailor your writing for different audiences. By reading such reports, you gain a strategic advantage, allowing you to anticipate and adapt to changes before they become mainstream.

Participating in AI Communities

Being part of an AI community is not just about learning but also about professional growth. Engaging with others who share your interest in AI provides opportunities to exchange knowledge, solve problems collaboratively, and a sense of community that can keep you motivated and inspired in your freelance writing journey.

Online Forums

Online forums such as Reddit's r/MachineLearning, Stack Overflow, and specialized AI groups on LinkedIn offer platforms for discussing AI-related topics. By joining these forums, you can make inquiries, share bits of knowledge, and acquire insights from others. This sense of community and collaboration can make you feel supported and part of a more extensive network, enhancing your professional growth.

For example, you might come across a discussion about the best AI tools for content generation. Participating lets you discover new tools like Jasper or Copy.ai, which can streamline your writing process. Participating in these forums helps you build a network of peers who can support your freelance journey.

Professional Networks

Joining professional networks like the Association for the Advancement of Artificial Intelligence (AAAI) or local AI clubs can provide access to exclusive resources, events, and training opportunities. These networks frequently organize conferences, workshops, and webinars where leading professionals convey their wisdom.

Through these networks, you might attend a webinar on the latest trends in AI-driven content creation, gaining insights that you can immediately apply to your work. Engaging with professionals in these networks can also lead to collaborations, opening up new avenues for your freelance business.

Keeping up with AI innovations requires a dedication to constant learning and growth. You ensure your skills and knowledge remain cutting-edge by staying updated with AI trends through news sources industry reports, and participating in AI communities. Taking this proactive approach enhances your freelance writing skills and establishes you as a forward-thinking professional in the industry. Next, we'll examine the benefits of attending AI conferences and workshops.

Attending AI Conferences and Workshops

Joining AI workshops and conferences can immensely improve your freelance writing career. These events provide insights into the latest AI trends, tools, and best practices, helping you stay ahead in the competitive field. You'll gain practical knowledge, network with industry leaders, and engage in collaborative learning experiences. This potential for personal growth and career advancement can inspire and motivate you to take your writing to the next level.

Major AI Events

Attending major AI events can significantly boost your freelance writing career. Annual AI conferences and specialized workshops offer a wealth of knowledge and networking opportunities. Engage with industry leaders, explore cutting-edge technologies, and gain practical insights to enhance your writing process. Let's dive into these valuable learning experiences.

Annual AI Conferences

Annual AI conferences are a goldmine of information and networking opportunities. Events like the AI Summit, NeurIPS, and the World AI Conference bring together top AI minds from around the globe. Attending these conferences provides an exhaustive overview of AI's current and future trends.

For instance, at the AI Summit, you can attend keynote sessions from industry leaders, participate in panel discussions, and explore exhibitions featuring cutting-edge AI technologies. NeurIPS, known for its focus on machine learning and computational neuroscience, offers workshops and tutorials that delve into the technical aspects of AI, providing a deeper understanding of the algorithms and methodologies that drive AI advancements.

These conferences often feature sessions tailored explicitly to AI's role in creative fields like writing. For example, a workshop on AI in content creation can demonstrate how to leverage AI tools to generate engaging blog posts or optimize SEO. You'll learn from experts who share their experiences and case studies, offering practical insights to apply to your freelance writing projects.

Specialized Writing and Tech Workshops

In addition to large-scale conferences, specialized workshops on writing and technology can be incredibly beneficial. Often smaller and more interactive, these workshops provide opportunities for hands-on learning and personalized feedback.

For example, a workshop might focus on specific AI tools to enhance your writing process. You'll experiment with tools like Grammarly, Hemingway, and GPT-based writing assistants in real time, learning how to use them to improve your writing efficiency and quality. Workshops often include breakout sessions where you can discuss challenges and share solutions with fellow writers, fostering a collaborative learning environment.

Moreover, tech workshops can teach you how to integrate AI into your marketing strategy. You'll learn to use AI to analyze market trends, predict audience preferences, and generate targeted content that resonates with your readers. These skills help freelance writers grow their services and draw more customers.

Networking Opportunities

Attending major AI events is essential for staying updated and enhancing your skills in freelance writing. Annual AI conferences and specialized workshops offer invaluable insights, networking opportunities, and hands-on experience with cutting-edge tools. Associate with industry leaders, stay educated about the latest advances and implement practical strategies to boost your writing career.

Meeting Industry Leaders

Meeting industry leaders is one of the most significant advantages of attending AI conferences and workshops. Top professionals from academia, industry, and government attend these events. Engaging with these experts can provide you with unique insights and inspiration.

For instance, you could attend a Q & A session with a leading AI researcher at an AI conference or participate in a roundtable discussion with AI entrepreneurs. These interactions can generate new ideas and give you valuable project feedback. Networking with industry leaders also opens doors for potential collaborations and mentorship opportunities, helping you grow your freelance writing career.

Collaborative Learning

Conferences and workshops are also excellent platforms for collaborative learning. Engaging with peers who share your interests and challenges can lead to fruitful collaborations and a deeper understanding of AI applications in writing.

For example, during a workshop breakout session, you might work with other freelance writers to solve a common problem, such as optimizing content for SEO using AI tools. This collaborative effort enhances your learning experience and builds a network of like-minded professionals who can support you in your freelance journey.

Furthermore, many conferences and workshops offer online communities and forums where you can continue the conversation and collaboration long after the event has ended. These communities provide helpful resources for keeping up with the latest AI and writing developments, conveying experiences, and pursuing guidance from other professionals.

Real-Life Success Stories

To illustrate the impact of attending AI conferences and workshops, consider the story of Jane, a freelance writer who participated in the AI Summit. Jane was initially hesitant about integrating AI into her writing process. Still, after attending a session on AI-driven content generation, she was inspired to experiment with AI tools.

Jane started using an AI writing assistant to help brainstorm and draft her articles. She used AI-powered SEO tools to enhance her content for search engines. As a result, Jane's productivity increased, and her articles began ranking higher on Google, attracting more clients and boosting her freelance business.

Similarly, another freelance writer, John, attended a specialized workshop on AI in content marketing. He used AI to analyze his audience's preferences and tailored his content accordingly. This personalized approach led to higher engagement rates and more satisfied clients, significantly enhancing John's reputation and client base.

Freelance writers gain numerous benefits from attending AI conferences and workshops. These events provide a wealth of knowledge, practical skills, and networking opportunities to help you stay ahead in the rapidly evolving field of AI. By engaging with industry leaders, participating in collaborative learning experiences, and applying the insights gained from these events, you can enhance your writing process, attract more clients, and achieve tremendous success in your freelance career.

As you explore these opportunities, you'll discover new tools and techniques to experiment with, paving the way for continued growth and innovation in your writing practice.

Experimenting with New Tools

Staying ahead of the curve is crucial in the fast-paced domain of freelance writing. Experimenting with new tools can significantly enhance your productivity and creativity. Whether it's beta testing cutting-edge AI software or integrating innovative applications into your workflow, embracing new technology can set you apart. Let's explore how you can experiment with these tools to maximize your freelance writing success.

Beta Testing AI Software

Beta testing AI software lets you be among the first to explore cutting-edge tools, offering firsthand experience and the chance to shape their development. By joining early access programs and providing valuable feedback, you can enhance these tools and position yourself as a thought leader in the freelance writing community.

Early Access Programs

Beta testing AI software allows you to be among the first to try out groundbreaking tools. Writers can often join early access programs to explore the latest advances in AI technology. Participating in these programs allows you to gain firsthand experience with tools that might revolutionize your writing process.

OpenAI frequently provides early access to new versions of its language models, allowing you to experiment with the latest features and give valuable feedback to the developers. This helps you understand the tool's potential and positions you as a thought leader in the freelance writing community.

Take the case of Jane, a freelance writer who joined an early access program for a new AI content generator. She discovered features that significantly cut down her research time. By sharing her insights with the developers, she contributed to refining the tool, which later became a staple in her writing arsenal.

Providing Feedback to Developers

Beta testing isn't just about using new tools; it's also about shaping their development. Providing feedback to developers is a crucial part of this process. Your insights can help improve the software, making it more effective for users like you.

When you test a new AI tool, prioritize its integration with your current workflow, functionality, and ease of use. Document your experiences and give feedback to the developers. Constructive feedback can lead to enhancements that directly benefit your work.

For example, during the beta testing of an AI editing tool, several freelance writers noticed the software struggled with context-specific grammar. Their detailed feedback prompted the developers to tweak the algorithms, resulting in a more reliable and context-aware editing tool.

Integrating Innovative Tools

Using innovative AI tools in your writing process can significantly improve productivity and ingenuity. By embracing emerging applications and customizing solutions tailored to your needs, you'll streamline your workflow and enhance the quality of your work. Let's examine how you can use these powerful tools to advance your freelance writing.

Emerging AI Applications

Integrating emerging AI applications into your writing process can open up new possibilities. These applications range from AI-powered research assistants to advanced content-generation tools. Incorporate these innovations to simplify your workflow and concentrate more on the creative facets of writing.

Consider using AI tools like Grammarly, which corrects grammatical errors and offers suggestions for style improvement. Another example is Jasper (formerly Jarvis), an AI that helps generate high-quality content based on brief inputs. Using these tools can improve both the quality and efficiency of your writing.

In one instance, Tom, a freelance writer, started using an AI-powered research assistant to gather data for his articles. This tool saved him hours of manual research, allowing him to allocate more time to crafting engaging narratives. As a result, his productivity soared, and he could take on more projects.

Custom Solutions for Writers

Every writer has unique needs; sometimes, off-the-shelf tools may not suffice. Creating custom AI solutions specifically tailored to your needs can transform your work. This involves customizing existing tools or developing new ones that cater to your workflow.

For example, if you frequently write SEO-optimized content, you might benefit from an AI tool that analyzes keyword trends and suggests relevant topics. By working with developers to create such a tool, you can ensure it fits seamlessly into your process and delivers the desired outcomes.

Another freelance writer, Sarah, collaborated with a developer to create a personalized content planning tool. This AI-driven solution helped her organize her writing schedule, track deadlines, and suggest content ideas based on her niche. The custom tool increased her efficiency and improved the quality of her work.

Practical Insights

Real-life success stories highlight how new tools can be transformative. For example, a freelance writer specializing in technical content, Emily integrated an AI-based plagiarism checker into her workflow. This tool ensured her work's originality and suggested paraphrasing complex technical jargon. As a result, her articles became more accessible to a broader audience, leading to increased client satisfaction and repeat business.

Similarly, John, a content strategist, used an AI tool to analyze the performance of his articles. He refined his content strategy by understanding which topics and styles resonated most with his audience, and he saw a significant boost in engagement and conversions.

Experimenting with new tools is crucial for maintaining a competitive edge in freelance writing. You can stay ahead of technical advances by beta testing AI software. Integrating innovative tools can streamline your workflow and enhance your productivity. Embracing these opportunities makes you a forward-thinking writer, ready to tackle the challenges of the digital age.

Next, let's explore how to build a personal AI toolkit that perfectly complements your writing needs.

Building a Personal AI Toolkit

A well-curated AI toolkit in freelance writing can mean the difference between thriving and surviving. Integrating essential AI tools into your workflow can enhance efficiency, boost creativity, and streamline processes. This guide will walk you through must-have applications, specialized tools for niche markets, and ways to customize your workflow to suit your personal preferences.

Curating Essential AI Tools

Creating a personal AI toolkit is crucial for boosting your productivity and creativity as a freelance writer. By incorporating versatile, must-have applications and specialized tools for niche markets, you can streamline your workflow, enhance your writing quality, and stay ahead of the competition. Let's explore the essential AI tools you need to succeed.

Must-Have Applications

To kick off your AI toolkit, you need a solid foundation of versatile tools that cater to various aspects of freelance writing.

- **Grammarly:** A favorite among many writers, Grammarly ensures your content is grammatically accurate and stylistically refined. It goes beyond a simple spell checker by offering advanced grammar tips, tone adjustments, and even plagiarism detection. According to a study by Grammarly, users report saving up to 20% of their time on writing tasks using this tool (*Unlocking Team Efficiency*, 2021).

- **Jasper:** Formerly known as Jarvis, Jasper is a powerful AI writing assistant that helps generate content for blogs, social media, and more. It's valuable for brainstorming ideas and crushing writer's block. Freelance writers appreciate Jasper for developing coherent and engaging text.

- ☐ **Frase:** Frase combines SEO research with AI writing to assist you in creating content that ranks excellently on search engines. It offers tools for topic research, SERP analysis, and content optimization, ensuring your articles are high-quality and discoverable.

- ☐ **QuillBot:** This tool excels in paraphrasing and rewording text, allowing you to rewrite content without losing its original meaning. It's invaluable for creating unique, plagiarism-free content and refining your writing style.

Specialized Tools for Niche Markets

Specialized AI tools can help you stand out if you're working within specific niches.

- ☐ **Copy.ai:** Perfect for marketing professionals, Copy.ai offers a library of templates for different types of content, including ads, emails, and social media posts. Its ability to create engaging and persuasive copy makes it ideal for marketing initiatives.

- ☐ **GrowthBar:** This tool improves SEO performance, offering features like keyword research, competitor analysis, and topic generation. It's a must-have for writers who want to boost their online visibility.

- ☐ **Sudowrite:** Tailored for creative writers, Sudowrite helps with brainstorming, developing plot points, and editing. It benefits novelists and short story writers looking to enhance their creative output.

Customizing Your Workflow

Building a personal AI toolkit can transform your freelance writing game, making your workflow smoother and more efficient. You can boost productivity and creativity by carefully selecting essential tools and customizing them to fit your needs. Let's explore how to build your ideal AI toolkit and enhance your writing process.

Personal Preferences

Personalizing your AI tools is crucial for maximizing their potential. Start by configuring the settings to match your writing style and workflow. For example, adjusting Grammarly's tone detector to align with your preferred style can ensure more accurate suggestions. Similarly, using Jasper's templates for your writing needs can save time and improve consistency.

- **Task Automation:** Tools like Zapier can automate repetitive tasks, such as posting new blog entries to social media. By integrating various apps, you can create workflows that streamline your daily activities, allowing you to focus more on writing.

- **Time Management:** Futurenda is an AI-powered productivity app that effectively manages your time by learning your habits and automatically creating a daily agenda, keeping you organized and on track.

Enhancing Efficiency and Creativity

To enhance efficiency and creativity, leverage AI tools that complement each other.

- **Collaborative Tools:** Platforms like Google Workspace or Microsoft 365 integrate AI to suggest real-time edits and improvements. These tools enable seamless collaboration, helping you work efficiently with clients and colleagues.

- **Mind Mapping:** Use tools like MindMeister or XMind to visualize brainstorming and arranging your ideas. When paired with AI writing assistants, these tools can transform initial ideas into fully fleshed-out articles.

- **Content Analysis:** Tools like the Hemingway App can analyze your writing for readability, highlighting complex sentences and suggesting simpler alternatives. This ensures your content is accessible and engaging for a wider audience.

- **SEO Optimization:** Besides Frase, tools like SurferSEO provide in-depth analysis and recommendations for optimizing your content for search engines. These insights help you boost your content's visibility and reach.

Building a personal AI toolkit tailored to your freelance writing needs can revolutionize your workflow. By curating essential applications, incorporating specialized tools for niche markets, and customizing your setup to enhance efficiency and creativity, you'll be well-equipped to tackle any writing project. As AI technology evolves, staying updated with the latest tools and trends will ensure you remain competitive and productive in the ever-changing freelance writing landscape.

Key Takeaways

- Personalizing AI tools enhances effectiveness by aligning settings with your writing style and workflow.

- Task automation tools handle repetitive tasks efficiently, giving you more writing time.

- Collaborative tools enable you to make real-time edits and improvements.

- Mind mapping tools help organize thoughts visually and develop ideas into articles.

- Content analysis tools improve readability by simplifying complex sentences.

- SEO optimization tools provide in-depth analysis and recommendations to increase content visibility.

- Curating essential AI tools is crucial for a productive writing toolkit.

- Specialized tools cater to niche markets and enhance specific writing tasks.

- Staying updated with AI trends and integrating innovative tools ensures competitiveness and productivity in freelance writing.

Building your personal AI toolkit is a game-changer in freelance writing. By curating the right tools and customizing your workflow, you'll boost productivity and creativity, making your writing process more efficient and enjoyable. Stay informed about AI advancements to keep your competitive advantage in this continually developing industry.

Conclusion

Reflecting on your AI journey, which refers to learning and integrating AI tools into your writing process, and seeing how far you've come is incredible. You started with the basics, exploring the transformative power of AI in freelance writing. From understanding the core concepts of artificial intelligence to integrating these tools into your daily workflow, you've significantly enhanced your productivity and creativity.

Throughout this book, we've covered many tools and techniques. You've learned about essential AI writing assistants like Grammarly and ProWritingAid, which help polish your grammar and style by providing real-time suggestions and corrections. Content generation tools like Jasper and Writesonic have become your go-to for creating engaging blog posts and social media content, offering a variety of templates and ideas to spark your creativity.

Research and data analysis has been made easier with AI-powered tools like Google Scholar and Semantic Scholar, allowing you to incorporate rich data into your writing effortlessly. Additionally, with AI integrations, such as Trello and Asana, project management tools have streamlined your organizational tasks, ensuring you stay on top of your deadlines and goals by automating reminders and task assignments.

We've explored success stories and case studies highlighting AI's significant impact on freelance writing careers. For example, writers like Jane, who used AI to boost her productivity and client engagement by automating repetitive tasks and improving the quality of her writing, and John, who optimized his content strategy through AI tools by analyzing data and generating content ideas, showcase these technologies' potential. These instances illustrate and confirm the real benefits of adopting AI.

Your personal growth and achievements throughout this journey are truly commendable. You've conquered initial challenges, such as adapting to new workflows and troubleshooting technical issues. Every milestone, no matter how small, showcases your dedication and hard work. You've made significant strides in your freelance writing career by mastering new tools and successfully automating repetitive tasks. Take a moment to appreciate your accomplishments, reflecting your determination and resilience.

Looking ahead, the future of AI in writing is brimming with possibilities. Staying informed about industry trends ensures you stay ahead of the curve. Advancements in AI are continuously emerging, offering new opportunities for writers. For instance, developing more sophisticated natural language processing algorithms promises more accurate and creative AI-generated content. By staying informed about these trends, you can use cutting-edge tools effectively and keep your competitive edge.

Preparing for future changes involves adapting to technological shifts and continuously developing your skills. The landscape of AI and writing is ever-evolving, and your willingness to learn and adapt will ensure your success. Invest time in training resources, online courses, and community forums to keep your skills and knowledge up-to-date. Additionally, consider subscribing to AI and writing newsletters, following industry experts on social media, and attending webinars and conferences to stay informed about the latest trends and developments in AI.

Continued exploration is crucial. Maintaining a growth mindset and committing to lifelong learning will keep you innovative and curious. Engage with the AI community, share your knowledge and experiences, and contribute to discussions about AI in writing. This active participation will enhance your understanding and help shape the future of AI applications in creative industries.

As you move forward, remember to balance creativity and technology. AI tools are powerful allies, but your unique voice and perspective as a writer remain irreplaceable. Leveraging AI for success and fulfillment means integrating these technologies to enhance, not overshadow, your creative process. Remember, AI tools complement but do not replace human creativity and judgment. They can assist in various aspects of writing, but the final output should always reflect your unique style and voice.

Your role in shaping the future of writing isn't just significant; it's pivotal. By embracing AI and inspiring others to explore its potential, you are part of a broader movement toward innovative and efficient writing practices. Your journey sets a precedent for future writers, demonstrating that integrating AI into your workflow is not just feasible; it's gratifying. You are not just a writer; you are a pioneer, and your contributions are shaping the future of writing.

In conclusion, embracing an AI-enhanced writing career opens up possibilities. The knowledge and skills you've gained position you as a forward-thinking professional ready to tackle the challenges and opportunities that lie ahead. Stay curious, keep learning, and explore AI's endless possibilities to enhance your writing career. Your journey with AI is just beginning, and the future holds exciting prospects for those willing to innovate and adapt. Take the first step today by integrating one new AI tool into your writing process and see the difference it can make.

About the Author

Florence De Borja is a seasoned professional who blends deep tech expertise with the power of words. With over 15 years of experience in the IT industry and 14 years as a freelance writer, Florence brings a rare combination of technical insight and creative skill to every project she takes on.

Her career began in the fast-evolving world of information technology, where she built a solid foundation in systems, software, and digital tools. But it was through writing that she found her true voice. From tech blogs to in-depth guides, Florence has written across various topics, helping brands and individuals communicate with clarity and impact.

In *The AI Freelancer: Leveraging Artificial Intelligence to Boost Your Writing Career*, Florence shares the strategies, tools, and mindset shifts that helped her thrive in a competitive industry—especially in a world where AI is reshaping our work. Her approach, which is not only practical but also honest, is rooted in years of real-world experience navigating technology and the freelance landscape, providing readers with a sense of reassurance and confidence.

Today, Florence mentors aspiring writers, consults with digital teams, and continues to explore how human creativity can work alongside AI. Her strong belief in the power of adaptability, lifelong learning, and doing meaningful work on your terms is not just a personal philosophy but a source of encouragement and optimism for all who seek to grow and succeed in their careers.

References

AlphaGo. (n.d.). Google DeepMind. https://deepmind.google/technologies/alphago/

Artificial intelligence - Alan Turing, AI Beginnings. (n.d.). Britannica.
    https://www.britannica.com/technology/artificial-intelligence/Alan-Turing-and-the-
    beginning-of-AI

Babich, N. (2023, June 4). *Explained: the F-shape pattern for reading content.* Writeful.
    https://writefulcopy.com/blog/f-shaped-pattern-explained

Beccue, M., & Kaul, A. (2019, April 16). *Tractica report: Natural language processing for the
    rnterprise.* ITPro Today. https://www.itprotoday.com/artificial-intelligence/tractica-report-
    natural-language-processing-enterprise

Bello, C. (2024, January 20). *The best AI tools to power your academic research.*
    Euronews.com. https://www.euronews.com/next/2024/01/20/best-ai-tools-academic-
    research-chatgpt-consensus-chatpdf-elicit-research-rabbit-scite

Belyh, A. (2023, January 11). *The ultimate list of CRM statistics for 2024.* FounderJar.
    https://www.founderjar.com/crm-statistics/

Bersin, J. (2023, March 7). *New MIT research shows spectacular increase in white collar
    productivity from ChatGPT.* Josh Bersin. https://joshbersin.com/2023/03/new-mit-
    research-shows-spectacular-increase-in-white-collar-productivity-from-chatgpt/

The big list of content marketing statistics. (n.d.). Brafton. https://www.brafton.com/content-
    marketing-statistics/

Chui, M., Manyika, J., Bughin, J., Dobbs, R., Roxburgh, C., Sarazzin, H., Sands, G., &
    Westergren, M. (2012, July). *The social economy: Unlocking value and productivity
    through social technologies.* McKinsey.
    https://www.mckinsey.com/~/media/mckinsey/industries/technology%20media%20and%
    20telecommunications/high%20tech/our%20insights/the%20social%20economy/mgi_the
    _social_economy_executive_summary.pdf

Cybersecurity research: All in one place. (2024, April 13). Cybercrime Magazine.
    https://cybersecurityventures.com/research/

The development of the automatic writing machine: The typewriter. (n.d.). Encyclopedia.com.
    https://www.encyclopedia.com/science/encyclopedias-almanacs-transcripts-and-
    maps/development-automatic-writing-machine-typewriter

4 accounts payable statistics to know in 2021. (n.d.). MineralTree.
    https://www.mineraltree.com/blog/accounts-payable-statistics/

Gifford, J. (2021, August 10). *52/17 updated: longer work time and breaks*. DeskTime. https://desktime.com/blog/52-17-updated-people-are-now-working-and-breaking-longer-than-before

Grammarly named the leading ai writing assistant in G2 Fall Grid® reports. (2023, October 11). Business Wire. https://www.businesswire.com/news/home/20231011468441/en/Grammarly-Named-the-Leading-AI-Writing-Assistant-in-G2-Fall-Grid%C2%AE-Reports

Heshmart, S. (2021, September 23). *5 tips to improve concentration with music*. Psychology Today. https://www.psychologytoday.com/gb/blog/science-choice/202109/5-tips-improve-concentration-music

How to create a brand voice. (2021, September 9). Grammarly. https://www.grammarly.com/business/learn/how-to-create-a-brand-voice/

Inglis, J. (2018, August 11). *Re-typing history: The Sholes-Glidden typewriter and the QWERTY keyboard*. National Museums Scotland Blog. https://blog.nms.ac.uk/2018/08/11/re-typing-history-the-sholes-glidden-typewriter-and-the-qwerty-keyboard/

Joki, K. (2021, August 18). *Top 5 most frustrating writing mistakes (and how to avoid them)*. Grammarly. https://www.grammarly.com/blog/top-5-most-frustrating-writing-mistakes-and-how-to-avoid-them/

Kandi, T., Kelly, J., & Brinker, M. (2024, February 21). *Are your content creation workflows AI ready?* Deloitte Digital. https://www.deloittedigital.com/us/en/insights/perspective/ai-ready-content-creation.html

Kasumovic, D. (2024, May 6). *Digital marketing benchmark report 2024*. Influencer Marketing Hub. https://influencermarketinghub.com/digital-marketing-benchmark-report/

Korolov, M. (2024, March 13). *3 areas where gen AI improves productivity — until its limits are exceeded*. CIO. https://www.cio.com/article/1312721/3-areas-where-gen-ai-improves-productivity-until-its-limits-are-exceeded.html

Lieberman, M. (2014, January 20). *10 stats about inbound marketing that will make your jaw drop*. HubSpot Blog. https://blog.hubspot.com/insiders/inbound-marketing-stats

MacKay, J. (2019, January 24). *The state of work life balance in 2019 (According to data) - RescueTime*. RescueTime Blog. https://blog.rescuetime.com/work-life-balance-study-2019/

New Epsilon research indicates 80% of consumers are more likely to make a purchase when brands offer personalized experiences. (2018, January 9). Epsilon. https://www.epsilon.com/us/about-us/pressroom/new-epsilon-research-indicates-80-of-consumers-are-more-likely-to-make-a-purchase-when-brands-offer-personalized-experiences

Schwarz, L. (2022, May 25). *QuickBooks vs ERP: Choose the best solution*. NetSuite. https://www.netsuite.com/portal/resource/articles/accounting/quickbooks-vs-erp.shtml

2024 AI content marketing report for SMBs. (n.d.). Semrush. https://www.semrush.com/goodcontent/ai-content-marketing-report/

Typewriter. (n.d.). New World Encyclopedia. https://www.newworldencyclopedia.org/entry/Typewriter

Unlocking team efficiency with Grammarly business analytics. (2021, April 27). Grammarly. https://www.grammarly.com/business/learn/unlocking-team-efficiency/

Virgillito, D. (2022, September 15). *Slack: What is it & why do startups adore it?* Elegant Themes. https://www.elegantthemes.com/blog/resources/slack-what-is-it-why-do-startups-adore-it

Winn, Z. (2023, July 14). *Study finds ChatGPT boosts worker productivity for some writing tasks*. MIT News. https://news.mit.edu/2023/study-finds-chatgpt-boosts-worker-productivity-writing-0714